Strip Tees

Strip Tees

A Memoir of Millennial
Los Angeles

Kate Flannery

Henry Holt and Company
New York

Henry Holt and Company
Publishers since 1866
120 Broadway
New York, New York 10271
www.henryholt.com

Henry Holt® and ⒽⒽ® are registered trademarks of Macmillan Publishing Group, LLC.

Library of Congress Cataloging-in-Publication Data is available.

ISBN: 9781250827289

Our books may be purchased in bulk for promotional, educational, or business use. Please contact your local bookseller or the Macmillan Corporate and Premium Sales Department at (800) 221-7945, extension 5442, or by e-mail at MacmillanSpecialMarkets@macmillan.com.

First Edition 2023

Designed by Meryl Sussman Levavi

Printed in the United States of America

10 9 8 7 6 5 4 3 2 1

Author's Note: This is a true story, though some names and details have been changed.

For my sister

Strip Tees

Prologue

I was in Los Angeles for less than a month before I got scouted by a cult. It was autumn of 2004, and I was twenty-three—prime cult age.

It didn't happen the way I would have expected. It didn't involve a free-loving Manson type with a flower in his beard, or a wild-eyed Marshall Applewhite pitching a UFO ride on a comet. Freak daddies like that were easy to spot—they'd never catch me. I was fresh out of Bryn Mawr, a women's college back East, well trained in feminist ideology. I knew I could spot a bad man a mile away.

But it was just a girl who approached me. Someone like me. I didn't suspect a thing.

III

The Glendale Galleria was my kind of mall. Not the Beverly Center, not the Grove, not any mall where Cher Horowitz would have shopped. Those places were packed with the pricey Y2K styles of the day that made me cringe—bedazzled Ed Hardy tees, distressed Diesel jeans, Von Dutch trucker hats. Expensive, tattoo-themed clothing I associated with dorky rocker dads or rich kids searching for a personality. Flashy brands and logo worship only communicated how much money a person had. Paying to be an advertisement was for suckers. I had too much fashion ingenuity for that.

But the Glendale Galleria was a mall for the proletariat. It didn't put on airs. It had a Payless, a Mervyn's. It was a fashion destination for people on a budget—my people.

I rolled down the escalator into its sacred depths.

Inside the Galleria it was dark and dank, with fountains and foliage unchanged from the 1980s. I instantly knew it—an old friend—despite having never stepped foot inside, and the loneliness that had been haunting me all day lifted in an instant. Even though I was two thousand miles from it, I was home.

I had just moved from Philly, and I didn't know a soul. My new life was feeling so empty, I needed cheap stuff to fill it up, and there was something particularly alluring that drew me to the Galleria that day—a store I had heard about that was becoming ubiquitous in Los Angeles, popping up faster than a rash of Starbucks in the cityscape.

It was a fast-fashion empire to rule them all—pitch-perfect knock-offs of designer styles on an endlessly rotating trend carousel that changed out daily. If you couldn't afford a Murakami Louis Vuitton monogram bag or the Miu Miu pleated micro mini, you could pacify yourself with their bogus cousins for a fraction of the price, and not feel bad tossing them when the trends shifted in a month or two.

I spotted the store's golden logo overhead.

Forever 21.

The name alone was pure poetry written in the California sand.

Forever 21—like the spirit of a roller-skating bikini girl riding into the Venice Beach dusk. *Forever 21*—like Madonna, like Angelyne— faces and bodies sculpted into youthful approximations of their aging corporal forms. *Forever 21*—the true spirit of Los Angeles. I felt it enter me, I was possessed.

I spotted it up ahead. I was close now. Only one barrier stood between us.

A lady in a white smock stepped in my path and fired a stream of perfume from a glittery pink bottle.

"Britney Spears's *Fantasy*, dear girl?"

"No!" I cried. An aerosol mist smelling like cupcakes hazed down around me.

Leave me alone, lady. Forever awaits!

I could see the glimmering storefront ahead, I was practically skipping now. I imagined all my new outfits waiting for me in there, future iterations of myself to try on for size. My eyes were so focused on the prize, I didn't see the girl up ahead. I nearly collided with her.

"Excuse me," she said, smiling a friendly smile, resting her hand lightly on my shoulder.

I turned around to face her.

She was wearing a college sweatshirt that said NORTHRIDGE across the front. Her swishy blond hair fell to her shoulders, and her pink face glowed in a freshly scrubbed way. She had on Levi's and pastel Sauconys, and her big smile instantly disarmed me.

"Hi," I said, returning her smile, waiting to hear what she needed. Directions, maybe? I stood up a little taller—only two weeks in LA and I was already getting mistaken for a local, one of those mythic California girls they write songs and movies about. This was going to be a real piece of—

"I have a prophecy for you," the girl said, interrupting my fantasy.

A prophecy? Here, by the Sunglass Hut?

Was she joking? For a second I was jolted back to middle school—was this girl bullying me? Messing with me while her giggling friends watched from the shadows?

But the girl wasn't laughing. Just smiling that wide toothpaste grin at me.

"It's about the Mothergod," she said.

I looked into her eyes, then, for the first time.

She held my stare like it belonged to her.

In that moment, everything about this normal girl melted away. Her eyes were completely empty, and as deep and black as a vortex. I couldn't see a *real* girl in there. And her smile wasn't friendly, as I had first thought. It was dreamy and unhinged. It disconnected itself from the hollowness of her stare.

A slow tingle started at the tips of my ears and coursed down my body. I was frozen there, glued to the industrial-grade linoleum. I opened my mouth to say something, but couldn't find the words.

She crept in closer.

I realized my silence was encouraging her, making her think I was interested.

"Do you *know* the Mothergod?" she asked, staring me down with those zombie eyes.

My brain kicked into action then, finally. It furiously computed the facts.

The Mothergod.

A prophecy.

A . . . *cult!*

Reality blasted back into view, the tableau of normal mall life unchanged around me. An instrumental version of the Spice Girls' "Say You Will Be There" was pumping through the overhead speakers. A snatch of a conversation from two women wearing name tags floated by. The perfume lady was still there, squirting passersby.

Everyone was going about their regular lives, unaware of the Mothergod and the cult girl and her hand on my shoulder. It felt like a two-ton weight, holding me there.

Back at Bryn Mawr, I learned what to do if some pervert's following you—you make a lot of noise, you draw attention to yourself. The hall advisors handed out these silver whistles during freshman orientation with wholesome, out-of-touch instructions to fend off assault.

If you're feeling threatened,
   blow your whistle.
If you see someone being attacked,
   blow your whistle.
If you hear someone blowing their whistle,
   blow your whistle.

But I was not prepared for this. No one and no whistle was going to save me from this nice college girl. I had to figure this one out on my own.

I pulled away from her grip and power walked to the parking garage, looking over my shoulder the whole way, a deflated version of the girl who had strolled in. I never even made it to Forever 21 that day. For all my swagger, all my liberated-woman-in-a-new-city BS I had been pumping myself up with since I arrived, the experience rattled me. It was the first inkling of doubt I had that the world outside my feminist utopia of a Seven Sister college might not be as textbook as they had made it out to be.

As a woman I'm always scanning my environment for predators, but running in fear of another girl? That was a new one.

On the drive back home, I checked myself out in the rearview mirror.

I looked the same as any other girl in the mall that day. A pedestrian ponytail, my eyeliner beginning to smudge with the afternoon. But the cult girl had sniffed out my loneliness like a dog on a fox. How had she been able to tell so easily? Was my new-girl naivete *that* obvious—a vulnerability that shot from me like light off a mirror? I felt weak and exposed, like all my confidence had leaked out. I wasn't fooling anyone.

I started second-guessing all of my decisions about coming to Los Angeles without any real plans. Maybe I had made a terrible mistake. One thing was for sure—I was going to have to be more careful on my own. I couldn't let something like this happen again. I was lonely, but not lonely enough for the Mothergod.

III

A few months later I met Ivy. Instead of a prophecy, she held out a business card.

Come join our team, the card read. **American Apparel.**

I took it from her hand immediately.

1

≡

The Scout

Ivy found me at Little Joy, a dive bar on Sunset Boulevard I discovered on the night the Santa Ana winds arrived. They roared in like a supernatural force, knocking the power out in Echo Park, and I thought it might be spooky to explore my new neighborhood like that, out there in the blackness with the sounds of the swaying palm trees creaking overhead. The night *felt* electric, it cracked with possibilities. Winds like these just didn't exist back in Philly.

I've always been someone who goes out looking for an experience, which is really how I ended up in LA in the first place. I had spent the last year terminally bored, watching the clock tick backward at the Philadelphia headquarters of UrbanOutfitters.com. When I landed the copywriting job right after my 2003 graduation, I was practically pinching myself—working for a hipster fashion megalith like Urban would be a rocket launch into my brand-new career in fashion, *and* I'd get an employee discount at my favorite store. I had scored my dream job on my first shot, this career woman stuff was going to be a snap!

But when I arrived on my first day, I was led down a sterile hallway to an empty desk and filed away between two panels of sliding corkboard.

Office culture at Urban was as bland as the Lean Cuisines rotating in the microwave, and my boss was a woman so out of fashion her name was Beverly. And I wasn't exactly writing about haute couture here—I was cataloging a tacky array of offensive novelty gifts—a board game called Ghettopoly, a T-shirt that read, VOTING IS FOR OLD PEOPLE.

How was I going to thrive in this morally corrupt corporate wasteland for the next fifty years? I felt myself growing older by the minute, and I knew right away I had ended up in the wrong office, the wrong job, the wrong life.

When I heard of a friend who had just moved to Los Angeles and was looking for a roommate to split the rent, I saw an escape hatch materializing on the western horizon. I had never been to LA before, but the city wasn't a total stranger to me. I felt like I knew it already.

That summer of 2004, the Californication of America was in full swing. I watched real-life LA teenagers on *Laguna Beach*, and actors portraying them on *The O.C.* LA was Paris and Nicole's hometown on *The Simple Life*, and where Vanilla Ice cohabitated with Ron Jeremy on *The Surreal Life*. It was a glamorous fable of a city—in a state governed by the Terminator—a chaotic fantasyland of opportunity where everyone was young and no one wore biz-cas, and it was calling my name. I immediately started saving my checks.

And now that I was here, with these mysterious winds rattling the windowpane in my pitch-black $800-a-month bedroom, I knew I had made the right decision. Los Angeles was clearly the place for me, and an exciting future awaited me here. I could feel it.

There was only one problem—my finances.

After just a few months of scrounging for random freelance copywriting jobs that never lasted, the five thousand buffer I had saved up back at Urban was gone with the wind, too. The final blow had been the two-thousand down payment I handed over on a Honda stick shift in *fiji blue pearl* with crank windows, and now I had monthly $250 car payments and insurance to worry about. There was nothing left in my savings to keep me from the harsh reality of returning to Philly, back to my old job at Urban, which Beverly assured would still be waiting for me if I couldn't make it in LA.

"In case it doesn't work out," Beverly said, sympathetically.

I gritted my teeth and smiled politely, but I knew I was never going back to that corporate hellhole. I would do whatever it took to stay in LA.

The night I met Ivy, I was getting desperate.

III

I was just about to give up on my walk through the Santa Anas—the wind was warm like bathwater but stung my bare legs with grit—when I saw Little Joy up ahead. It was on the side of Sunset that had been spared by the windstorm and still had electricity, and the bar was a glowing oasis in the inky night.

The tinkle of glasses and murmur of happy voices grew louder the closer I got. A neon arrow pointed cheerily to the entrance— COCKTAILS.

I paused at the door.

I'd never ventured alone into a bar by myself before that night. I was used to roaming with a pack of girls; I didn't even like eating in the dining hall alone. But that night something—my fear of failing here, my boredom, my loneliness, the crazy winds, maybe?—something was urging me to enter.

I handed over my Pennsylvania ID to the bouncer, who barely glanced at it, and stepped inside. The bar smelled like yesterday's cigarettes and the floor stuck gummily to my sneakers. There were a couple pool tables in the back, enshrouded in smoke. The Strokes' "The Modern Age" blasted from the jukebox, and a quick visit to the bathroom to fix my windblown hair revealed stalls full of chatty girls sharing cocaine and Parliaments. It reminded me of a dive back home, and I felt instantly comfortable.

I ordered a can of Tecate—an alien beer to me, but what everyone else was having—and settled at a barstool to try and meld into my surroundings.

It didn't work. I felt her eyes on me right away.

I turned to see a girl my age staring at me, sunglasses still perched atop her head even though the sun had set hours ago. She was smiling at me like she knew me already, and she had the kind of frizzy, curly hair that I associated with nerdy efficiency, which made me want to trust her. She looked like someone I'd know back home, someone from school. So when she gave me a little wave, I waved back, automatically.

She was sitting at a table with a couple other girls, and she was wearing a gold racerback tank that shone like an aura off her skin and a pair of matching short shorts. It was just basic gym wear at first glance, but something about that matching set looked special to me. It was vaguely vintage, something that would be at home on both a 1970s Olympian and a 1970s porn star, but still seemed new and fresh—it stuck out in the grungy bar that was marked over with tattoos and shredded rocker tees and the whale tails of thongs cresting over the asses of low-rise jeans.

I noticed the other girls sitting with her were wearing the same clean, classic athleisure wear. Brandless, like it belonged on everyone. Where did they even find this stuff? There had been nothing like it at the Galleria.

When the curly-haired one turned her wave into a come-hither, I hopped off my stool and headed over. I was intrigued by these special girls. What did they want with me?

"Hi, I'm Ivy," she said, holding out a card.

It looked like a business card, but it wasn't made of quality cardstock. It was just a slip of printer paper, curling at the edges and cut into an uneven rectangle by someone in a hurry. Xeroxed on the front of it was a picture of a girl in a bikini and a pair of striped athletic socks. She was high kicking over a block of text.

American Apparel, it read.

That name—it sounded so familiar. Sort of nebulous in its general-ness, almost generic-sounding. Had I heard it somewhere before, or just thought I had?

I took the card from her hand and scanned the rest.

A progressive, provocative retailer

   and manufacturer of knit T-shirts

Not dominated by logos

   or politically correct tribalism

Sweatshop free

Great travel opportunities

I flipped the card over.

Come join our team, it said.

Everything began to swim with meaning.

A retailer

A team, an opportunity

A . . . job!

I looked at Ivy, my heart pounding in my ears. This girl was my savior in hot shorts. How did she know this was just what I needed? It was pure serendipity, and I couldn't believe how fate had just handed over—

"I was thinking you could model for us," Ivy said.

Modeling?

I snapped back into reality and felt all my excitement deflate like an old balloon. I had watched three seasons of *Top Model* by that winter of 2005—Tyra teasing modeling careers on the end of a fishing line, yanking them away if the girls had the wrong teeth or the wrong body or the wrong personality. I was too smart to fall into that sexist trap after four years at Bryn Mawr. And I was a brain, not a beauty, couldn't she tell? I needed an actual *job* that would give me a paycheck every week, health insurance, a 401(k).

I tried to explain.

"I'm not a model, I'm a . . ."

I searched for the right word.

". . . a *feminist*."

Ivy laughed.

"You can be both, you know," she said, gesturing to the other girls at the table. They were all staring at me now, and I shifted self-consciously in my Converse.

"This isn't just a modeling job," Ivy assured me. "We do it all. You wanna hear about it?"

I sat down at their table. I had nothing to lose.

III

Ivy bought me and the girls another round of Tecates and started explaining.

American Apparel had started off simply as a T-shirt company, selling wholesale to anyone who might need a supply of blank tees for their band or business. But these weren't just any typical T-shirts—they were slim cut, European style. They clung sexily to your body, a stylish departure from the square tees of the 1990s that turned your torso as boxy as a LEGO.

The company couldn't make them fast enough. Boxes of the tees were flying out of the Factory as quick as they could be manufactured, and now the brand was expanding into retail. The new brick-and-mortar American Apparel stores were starting to race across the country faster than California wildfire. The company was so successful—growing at such breakneck speed—it was having trouble keeping up with itself.

"We have to wear lots of hats here," Ivy said.

She told me the same girls managing and working in the retail shops were also the same girls back in the headquarters designing the newest styles. And they were also the ones hiring all the new employees and scouting for new locations in cities where the company would be sure to thrive. And so it only made sense that they were also the campaign girls—the models—appearing in all the ads.

"We're more like spokesmodels," Ivy said, clarifying. "We're the face of the company because we're the ones running it."

When she put it like that, it didn't sound too bad. I could get down with being a spokesmodel, as long as it came with a regular paycheck.

This whole egalitarian system was the vision of the company's founder—a man with a mystical-sounding name.

Dove, Ivy said. Like the bird, maybe?

"He has some crazy ideas," Ivy said, her pretty face twisting with a smile. But he was committed to a better life for all of his employees, while also committed to turning a profit. Everything produced in the Factory was made by fair-wage workers, garments you could feel good about wearing and selling.

"Not like that Forever 21 fast-fashion garbage, made in sweatshops overseas," Ivy said, her nose wrinkling in disgust. "He knows you don't have to stand on people's necks to make a profit."

I felt a wave of guilt run through me. I was one of the masses mindlessly buying it. Of course the cheap stuff came at a great cost, I just wasn't the one paying it.

"American Apparel is different from all the rest because our boss isn't trying to cheat anyone," she said.

The girls at the table nodded in agreement.

"He's still a businessman, of course. Still a capitalist, just doing it ethically."

Ethical capitalism? Was there such a thing?

Ivy clocked the look on my face.

"Come see for yourself," she said. She invited me to meet her at the Factory the next morning, pointed an unpolished fingernail at the address listed on the bottom of the card:

747 Warehouse St.

"I'll give you the tour," she said. "And then you can decide if it's right for you. But as soon as I saw you I knew—you're one of us."

She wrapped her arm around my shoulder and pulled me in to her, smelling like Coppertone and jasmine. It was the first hug I had gotten since I'd arrived in the city three months ago, and I needed it. The way Ivy was looking at me told me that I had finally made a friend here.

On the walk home that night, I started to feel all my good old confidence coming back. A perfectly progressive job had fallen right into my lap when I needed it most. What had I been so worried about? I only needed to rely on myself, and I would always be okay. That was the women's college way, after all. I was going to make it here in LA.

You're one of us, Ivy had said.

For the first time since I arrived in this new city, I wasn't feeling lonely anymore. I felt like I was exactly where I was supposed to be.

I was in, in, in.

2

The Factory

The Factory sat back from Alameda Street, hidden from the road by a chain-link fence woven with orange bougainvillea. I drove right past the entrance—the unassuming opening in the hedge was easy to overlook—and I had to turn back around to find it. I double-checked my MapQuest print-out and slipped the card Ivy gave me back into my wallet. This was the place.

Once I saw it for the first time, I'd never miss it again. The official headquarters and manufacturing center for American Apparel was a hulking warehouse painted millennial pink, and it poked out of the craggy wedge of no-man's-land between the Fashion District and Skid Row like a determined flower.

Emblazoned across the top was a huge banner that read:

AMERICAN APPAREL IS AN INDUSTRIAL REVOLUTION

On the east side of the building, the message echoed in Spanish:

AMERICAN APPAREL ES UNA COMPAÑÍA REBELDE

Just reading it made my heart beat faster. I knew my future—the exciting one I was always meant to have—waited for me inside. I pressed hard on the gas pedal and zoomed through the unpaved lot, cranking up my window when a rising cloud of red dust threatened to infiltrate my car and grunge up the outfit I had agonized over all morning.

What to wear to the Factory?

The name, so Warholian. Loaded with instant mythos. It would have to be something simple, but special, like the classic Cali style that Ivy and the girls were wearing at the bar. I rummaged through every piece of clothing I owned, trying to find something that passed, but every item had a screen print, a lace appliqué, a bedazzlement somewhere, ruining everything. In the end I settled on a black cami I usually wore to sleep, and paired it with maroon surf shorts that were so tight you could see my middle name. They'd do. If I looked in the mirror and squinted, I might have passed for an American Apparel girl.

But there was still something so *ordinary* about my look. Something was missing.

I immediately thought of the hat.

It was a classic black felt floppy with a little bit of white contrast stitching along the band. It had been my mom's in the 1960s and now it was mine, a little connection between me and her all the way out here. As the youngest, I got all the hand-me-downs. My mother had a practicality so baked in, she even passed down her own initials to me so nothing with a monogram would go to waste—a bunch of old-fashioned jewelry and embroidered cloth handkerchiefs I never had much use for.

But the hat was cool, just my style. I had worn it on the plane so the crown wouldn't get crushed in my suitcase and it made the journey intact, but I hadn't had it on much since I arrived. It was a statement piece, and now it had found its role—it was obviously the perfect thing to wear to the Factory. Vaguely vintage, but utilitarian in the LA sunshine. I was glad I had been smart enough to bring it along in the move.

I was ready now.

Everything was just right, or as right as I could make it, as I weaved a path through the haphazardly parked array of dented pickups and minivans on my way to the front doors of the Factory. The outdoor lobby was an old concrete weighing station with two giant elevators and a card table manned by a yawning security guard, unimpressed by my hat.

"I'm here to see Ivy," I told him.

"Take it to the top," he said. "Seventh floor."

I crowded in and peeked under my brim to check out the eclectic mix of garment workers and sleepy hipsters who filled the elevator, and did my best to be cool and blend in. But inside, I was fizzing with nerves.

I *had* to leave this Factory with a job offer. This was my shot—one last hurdle to clear before I could start living a real life in LA. My heartbeat was pounding in my ears as I stepped off the elevator into a sterile white hallway bookended by a set of orange doors. I checked my watch. I was right on time, but where was Ivy? I tried to distract myself by examining a series of Polaroid snapshots, blown up and pasted on the wall.

In them, a blond girl in red sweatpants and a triangle bikini top prowled a playground at night. In the first one, she's hanging down from the monkey bars, peeking back at the photographer. In the next, she's midspin on the merry-go-round, her hair caught in her mouth. In another, she's straddling a swing with an impish smile on her face, nose scrunched up, defiantly.

I recognized the look right away—the smile of a teenage girl up to no good. I could practically hear the lukewarm Zima bottles clanking in her backpack, the flick of the lighter igniting a swiped Capri from mom's purse.

I knew this girl because I *was* this girl, or at least I had been recently. There was something so honest about the shots—just a real-life girl going about the business of girlhood, not really *modeling*. She didn't even have any makeup on.

It was so simple, but it worked. I couldn't stop looking at her.

"That's Natalie," a voice said. "She's great, right? You'll find her roaming around here."

I turned to see Ivy, who had materialized by my side in a pair of pirate boots and leggings, her curly hair in a topknot stabbed through with a Bic.

"Great hat. I *love*," she said.

I beamed as she leaned in for a hug. I was already off to a great start.

The elevator door opened again and unleashed another handful of employees ready to start their workday, all in head-to-toe American Apparel. A girl in Keds breezed by us in a cropped sweatshirt and a tennis skirt. I couldn't tell if she was channeling the 1950s, or a 1980s revival. All the looks were timelessly chic, their fashion inspirations hard to pin down.

"Let's start our tour with Retail Operations, the headquarters for the brand," Ivy said, swinging the orange door open into a clean white room with long conference tables and tall potted plants nodding toward the windows. A coffeemaker gurgled in a corner as a sea of beautiful employees opened laptops and unwound chargers, the room looking more like a Hollywood movie set than anything resembling the crummy office purgatory of Urban Outfitters.

What I noticed right away was that the whole operation appeared to be the veritable melting pot that my public high school had always promised America to be. Racial and cultural diversity fueled the creative nucleus of this brand—there were no old white guys in button-downs, not a single Boomer to be found. No one looked to be above the age of twenty-five, and I quickly clocked that the majority of the employees were young women.

Young women squinting at computer screens, dispensing orders, consulting with one another, rushing through with armfuls of swimwear, tags fluttering. Occasionally a few interloping guys would breeze through, wearing the same basic T-shirt in different colorways, practically interchangeable with each other, but it was obvious—women ruled here.

Ivy gestured across the room, and the Retail department began to transform before my eyes.

I realized I was looking at the corporate version of Bryn Mawr—a powerful woman behind every big desk. They orbited around the desk of one woman in particular, whose authority seemed to be radiating from the giant bun on top of her head.

"No, no, no," she screamed into her phone. "New York needs three thousand black bodysuits yesterday! Start making them tomorrow so we can start selling them by Friday afternoon."

Ivy looked at me and smiled, sensing my excitement. "That's Roz. Nothing gets made without her approval, she's a total genius."

Ivy and I hooked arms and continued our tour down to the fourth floor—one of the two floors devoted entirely to production—as she explained the mechanics of American Apparel's vertically integrated manufacturing system. Product development, design, marketing, and manufacturing, all were housed under the Factory's singular roof. That way, if a bikini had the wrong fit or fabrication, or wasn't quite the right shade of cerulean—"Or if something's a superseller, like Roz's black bodysuits," Ivy mentioned—production counts could be tailored accordingly, and the new products would be sold in stores immediately, while your competitors twiddled their thumbs, waiting months for a response from a foreign sweatshop on the other side of the world.

"It makes sense and it makes a profit," Ivy said.

It was truly brilliant—why didn't every factory operate like this instead of outsourcing jobs people already needed here in the States?

We stepped onto the fourth floor, a bright open space filled with windows and light, humming with sewing machines. Dozens of garment workers worked side by side in smooth choreography to create quivering piles of kelly-green men's underwear, which were quickly stacked up at the end of the assembly line. A new pair came into the world every ninety seconds.

I looked around and noticed sign-up sheets on the bulletin boards for free English lessons, and sign-out sheets for the company masseuse, on call to relieve any kinked necks or numb fingers that might flare up during the workday. I'd find out that at the end of each shift, tranquil spa music and a yoga routine in Spanish would warble from the speakers—a cool-down lap for the body and soul.

This was clearly no sweatshop.

I stared at the pile of green briefs, growing larger by the minute, and a thought occurred to me: *How would wearing this fair-wage underwear affect the people who wore it?*

Clothes harbor feelings, I knew from experience. I have dresses I wear when I want to feel worldly or sexy. A black turtleneck gives me the confidence of an eccentric genius. The right kind of leather moto jacket makes me invincible enough to tell a street harasser to fuck himself. And clothing retains memories, that was definitely true, too. I had sweaters I retired from my wardrobe because I'd been dumped in them, hoodies I'd donated because I had to send a pet over the Rainbow Bridge while wearing them. Some kind of emotional osmosis happens with clothes and the people who wear them, so it stands to reason that garments ethically manufactured are a wellspring of good vibes.

You feel good wearing them because someone felt good making them.

These undies were made by skilled laborers, compensated fairly for their efforts instead of being sucked dry by the capitalist parasite. There had to be good karma in buying ethical underwear like that. Maybe you'd spend the year that you wore them having satisfying sex, or at the very least avoid shitting your pants.

Maybe *that's* why this company was so successful and growing so rapidly. It was such a simple concept—treat your employees like human beings and be richly rewarded.

Suddenly a ruckus disrupted my daydream, disturbing the peaceful din on the floor.

The garment workers had stopped their work. Some of them were climbing up on their stools, clapping above their heads like they were at a concert. Some were still working, their hands flying along on autopilot, but their attention pulled to a corner of the room near the stairwell. All of them were cheering.

Out of a swinging door emerged a little man in a pair of aviator shades, bouncing with manic energy. He was high-fiving the outstretched hands of the workers closest to him, a flip phone pressed to one ear while another waited in a holster on his belt loop.

He was wearing a tight, white terry cloth polo and matching short shorts, thin as a piece of printer paper. Manicured muttonchops angled across his cheekbones beneath a mop of wavy brown hair. He looked like a 1970s carnival barker, or an extra from *Dazed and Confused*. He couldn't have been more than thirty-five, but an air of boyish buoyancy rolling off him made him seem much younger.

"WHAZZZUP?" he yelled, throwing his fist in the air. His other still held a phone firmly to his ear.

The workers cheered louder as he gave the air a few pumps. He stood still for a second or two, basking in the adulation, and then disappeared through the swinging door, gone as quickly as he came. Everyone quieted down and got off their stools, settling back in behind their stations, and soon the room filled again with the hypnotic hum of the sewing machines, an industrial lullaby.

"That's Dov," Ivy explained, but she didn't need to. I already knew this man had to be the ethical capitalist she'd told me about at Little Joy. And it seemed like everything she said about him *was* turning out to be true.

"He rides the city buses early in the morning and finds his workers on the way to their awful sweatshop jobs in the garment district, and he brings them here instead. How many CEOs do that?" Ivy said.

I tried to recall the CEO of Urban Outfitters—all I knew about him was that he was a Republican. But here, everyone seemed to know Dov, and everyone seemed to love him.

"Dov cares about all of us like that. We're a family here. Everyone works together for a common goal—to make the world a better place. This is a revolution," she said. "And not just a revolution in manufacturing, but a fashion revolution, a sex revolution. A revolution in advertising, industrialization, globalization!"

I hadn't ever heard anyone speak genuinely of a revolution. Apart from the time Gloria Steinem came to school to speak and what I'd heard on my parents' Beatles records, social revolutions seemed to live in the 1960s, resulting in the birth control pill and the Black Panthers.

But Ivy used the word "revolution" freely, setting it loose so that it was a real, live thing running around, and I was ready to revolt. Something radical was happening at this Factory, and I needed to be a part of it.

III

"Let's take some shots on the roof," Ivy said, a digital camera in one hand and mine in the other.

In all the morning's excitement, I'd forgotten that the reason Ivy had come up to me in the first place was to model for the company. All I had on my mind was where I would fit into this operation, what *my* job would be. I was hoping I'd be assigned a desk with the Amazonian women of the top floor, but Ivy said she had talked it over with Roz, and where I would be of most use would be at AA001, the Sunset Boulevard retail shop in Echo Park—the very first American Apparel store.

"You can help out Anarah," Ivy said. She explained that the

stressed-out store manager had a kid and needed someone to help her hold down the store.

I felt a seeping sense of disappointment, snuffing out all the exhilaration of my morning tour. Working retail felt like something I had outgrown and left behind in the last millennium like a pair of capri pants. I knew I could be so much more than just a shopgirl.

I tried to protest. "I have a degree," I told her, and instantly regretted it when I saw the look on her face.

"Oh, big whoop," she said, laughing. "Hard work is what will get you noticed here, not some piece of paper your parents paid for."

I could feel my face burn hot, I was too embarrassed to argue. She did have a point. I came looking for a job, and I'd leave with one—that was what was important here. I wanted to be a part of this company. I'd do whatever it took.

I agreed to work at the retail shop for $10.50 an hour, forty hours a week, minimum.

"But there's overtime," Ivy said. "Lots of it. Prove yourself at the Echo Park shop, and you'll move on to other roles quickly. What is it that you really want to do? Write? Take photos? Design clothing? Travel? Live abroad?" she asked.

All of these opportunities were available to me, if I put in the work now.

"Or you can go anywhere else, and pad the pockets of some greedy pig in a suit you'll never meet," Ivy said.

Her words stung, but I knew they were true. I hadn't told her about how soulless working for Urban had been, but she was describing my own experience back to me like a clairvoyant.

"Not at American Apparel. Here we hold each other up," Ivy said. "Here we'll change the world—together."

It was an exciting, inciting monologue I would come to know well, one I would soon memorize myself, one that was aptly nicknamed The Hustle, and one I could deliver with the passion of a hellfire minister at the drop of a hat. The first time I heard it was that day at the Factory, and I believed every word.

III

I was wearing all new clothes.

We had swung by Roz's desk to pick up a black velour romper with crisscross straps, a brand-new sample that hadn't hit the stores yet, and it needed to be shot today.

Roz was still shouting into her phone, barely noticing us. She was so tall she had to duck the midcentury light fixture swinging over her desk when she stood.

"Who says we can't?" she said.

A tinny voice stammered on the other end.

"We can, and *we will*," Roz shouted. "This is American Apparel, we can do . . . *anything we want*," she yelled into the phone, slamming it down into the receiver. I feared for whoever dared to tell Roz no.

Not me, I was obedient. I followed Ivy's instructions to change in a small dressing room around the corner, leaving my old outfit folded in a neat pile on the floor, my floppy hat on top. The romper fit great—it suited me so much better than what I had worn. Like all the other American Apparel styles I had seen that day, it, too, had a kind of fashion dichotomy. It looked like a bathing suit from the 1940s, but could double as a 1970s roller girl outfit.

The tag inside said, CLASSIC GIRL.

I checked myself out in the mirror and sized myself up.

Did I look like a model? Not exactly. But a Classic Girl? I could pass for one of them.

Ivy led me onto the roof, squinting at her Canon, fiddling with the settings. The camera looked expensive, and she didn't seem to know how to operate it.

"Shit, wait. How do I turn this flash off? Hold on a sec," she muttered, her brow furrowed with concentration.

I looked off to the downtown skyline, wavering behind me like a giant postcard.

Click click click.

Ivy's camera started snapping away.

"No, wait, I'm not ready!" I squealed. I hadn't even been looking, hadn't known we had started. But when Ivy flipped the camera around, I was surprised to see what a nice shot it really was. I was leaning against the wall, my face propped in my hands, not looking tense or self-conscious at all.

And I did look pretty great in the skimpy romper, second-wave feminism be damned. Its high cut made my skinny legs look a mile long on camera, and it felt natural to have my picture taken just the way I came—no makeup besides a little mascara, my hair just the way I did it back in the mirror at home.

"What's going to happen to these pictures?" I asked.

I wondered if I'd get posted up somewhere at the Factory like Natalie the playground girl, welcoming future visitors to the Factory from my spot high on the wall.

"Oh, they're just a test," Ivy said. "They'll go in the database, maybe get used for a hang tag, or the website. Maybe nothing at all. You'll be surprised how much you'll be getting your picture taken here," Ivy said. "Get used to it."

The shoot was over as quickly as it began. It was painless, really. Just a few snaps, nothing major. The last order of business was having my Polaroid taken—"Dov likes to see the new hires every week," Ivy said, waving the photo back and forth as it developed until a vision of me in the romper bloomed into frame.

With that Polaroid, it all became official. I was an American Apparel girl now.

Ivy gave me orders to report to the Echo Park shop the next afternoon, and I walked out of the Factory completely in awe of everything I had seen that day. I'd found a job, and it also felt like I had found a purpose—how strange to find both things in one place.

I crunched through the parking lot on the way back to my car, feeling every inch the American Apparel girl. The Factory's magic was a fog around me so thick that I didn't realize I was still wearing the velour romper until I was halfway home. All the clothes I had worn to the Factory—including my precious hat—were still stacked neatly up there in that dressing room on the seventh floor.

The hat I'd need to get back, but everything else could stay. That outfit was like the crusty old husk an insect leaves behind on a tree after it transforms, and I was ready to be rid of it.

3

The Girls

By some stroke of fate, the Echo Park shop was down the street from my apartment. I easily could have walked the few sun-bleached blocks down Sunset, where the sidewalk crawled with the spiky tongues of wild aloe plants and yucca stalks shot Jurassically out of the hillside. It was February, seventy-five degrees, and sunny. It would have been an idyllic walk to work, nothing like taking the Philly bus when I was back home.

But that first day, I was running late, of course. I had a long-standing habit of being ten minutes late that I'd cultivated the year before at Urban. I had good intentions every morning when I woke up, and I was still on track by the time I stepped out of the shower, but sometime between reheating my coffee for the third time and making sure the wings of my eyeliner were even, the clock started racing away from me. There was a reliability to my lateness—ten minutes, every day.

But after living here for just a few months, I was starting to see that California-time lagged behind so stonily, that it was *no worries* to be twenty minutes late. Now I was always ten minutes early. Without even realizing it, I was making a good impression.

In just a short time, California was changing me. And not just physically, although that was happening, too. My hair, which always frizzed up in the Philly humidity, laid down silkily in the dry desert air, and my acne cleared in the sunshine. On top of all that, I was an early girl now? I already liked myself better here.

I was seeing less and less of my roommate, who nailed down regular production assistant work on movie sets. He placed fastidious smoothie orders at Erewhon for picky starlets and loaded sodas into the catering fridge. He was becoming a ghost who haunted our apartment in the pre-dawn hours—the rattle of his Yellow Hornet energy pills would wake me out of a sound sleep as he left to start another eighteen-hour day.

The place felt lonely all by myself, but I was ready to fill it up with all the friends I was sure I'd make at my new job. I drove the few blocks to the shop, wearing the only American Apparel I owned—the velour romper I was wearing when I walked out of the Factory. When I called Ivy to ask about my hat, she assured me I'd get it back, *and* I'd get a monthly clothing allowance from here on out—new styles of whatever I wanted from the shop, whenever I needed it.

"It's the least we can do for an employee," Ivy said. "And Dov knows that nothing's better than a living, breathing advertisement. Take what you want."

At Urban, the company policy had been a 30 percent sales discount so a profit could be recouped on an employee purchase. It seemed so greedy, now that I'd seen the commercial symbiosis of the Factory. American Apparel's system was making more sense to me by the minute—take care of the ones who take care of you.

I was more excited than nervous as I parked on nearby Mohawk Street and walked down to Sunset, which was full of laundromats, discount evening gown shops, and *carnicerías* pumping delicious smells into the heat of the afternoon. This humble stretch of the road seemed to only share a name with the famous thoroughfare that came to mind when I'd thought of Sunset Boulevard before—the home of the Whisky a Go Go in the 1960s, the Viper Room in the 1990s, and the Standard Hotel at the turn of the millennium, where a model lounged in her underwear behind plexiglass in the lobby, a living art installation that doubled as a voyeur's delight.

On that glamorous side of the boulevard, the strip was lined with Gucci ads and Ferraris, and a giant Leonardo DiCaprio glowered down from billboards for *The Aviator*. But here, on the east side of town, a revolving sign for the Sunset Foot Clinic watched benevolently over the street—a cartoon foot smiling on one side, a sad foot on crutches wincing on the other. Coca-Cola ads on the bus benches were in Spanish, and mariachi music floated from the windows of Toyota work trucks, belching exhaust on their way downtown. The men hanging out of them made kissy noises as I walked by in my tiny romper while I did my best to pretend I couldn't hear them.

The traffic on that block of Sunset was as relentless as the sunshine, which glinted off the waiting cars at the Alvarado Street stoplight—a straight shot to the 5 freeway made this intersection one of the busiest in all the city. I noticed a huge billboard high over the corner, the perfect spot to grab the eye of the thousands of drivers who idled daily at the red.

The girl in the ad was lying on her side, caught in midlaugh, shooting a flirty look out at the world. She was wearing a pink-and-white baby rib halter top, which tied in a curlicue at the nape of her neck. Her wild, curly hair filled the rest of the frame.

My heart fluttered with recognition.

It was Ivy.

Definitely Ivy, reigning over the street chaos. High in the sky in an American Apparel ad, her face even larger than Leo's, even younger than his girlfriends'.

A flicker of pride ignited in me. I *knew* her. I stared for a few seconds, starstruck, before I noticed the arrow on the billboard pointing to a modest storefront below.

A simple black awning read:

AMERICAN APPAREL—MADE IN THE USA

I took a deep breath, pushed open the door, and stepped inside.

III

"I've been waiting for you," Anarah said. She had ruler-straight hair and silver braces, which made her seem like a teenager, but I could tell she was my age, maybe a year or two older. The keys jangling from the lanyard around her neck told me she was the one in charge here.

"I gotta pick up my kid in fifteen minutes, so I'm glad you're so early."

I checked my watch. I was right on time—a miracle.

"The other girls'll show up soon. You ever worked retail before?" she said, looping her bag over her shoulder.

I nodded. Plenty.

"Then you got this," Anarah said, sliding her sunglasses down from the top of her head.

"Wait!" I called after her. Was she going to just leave me here? Didn't I need some kind of training?

"How do I work the cash register?"

Anarah rolled her eyes at me.

"Ivy said you were smart. Figure it out."

She took the keys from around her neck and tossed them on the register, hurtling for the door. A gasp of hot desert air snuck in as it swung shut behind her.

Now I was all alone on the sales floor.

The store iPod kicked into Air's *Moon Safari* and retro French pop filtered down from the speakers.

So now what?

Ivy made it seem like Anarah would be grateful for the help, but she only seemed annoyed to see me. And now I was on my own, with no instructions other than *Figure it out.* This was sounding more like a reality TV challenge than a first day of work.

Was this some kind of test? Ivy and Anarah testing my competence, my ability to operate under pressure?

Ha! I thought. I'd show them. As a nerd, I've always loved tests—I knew I'd pass, I thrived under the academic pressure to succeed that had propelled me through my entire life. Running the cash register at a retail store would be an actual piece of cake. I checked out the sales system—a scanner gun, a credit card slider, a fully loaded cash drawer that popped out when I pressed ENTER. I knew how that all went.

I decided to take a walk around and familiarize myself with the layout of the tiny store, not much bigger than a two-car garage. A gradient rainbow of slim-cut unisex tees trailed the perimeter of the entire shop. These tees, style AA2001, retailed at $25 a pop—a price customers thought was either dirt cheap or outrageously expensive, I'd soon find out—and were the foundation of the wholesale empire that the retail division was building atop now.

I surveyed the men's section in a minute flat. It was just a tiny corner in the back, packed with hoodies, sweatpants, thermals, underwear. *Zzzzzz.* Nothing special here.

I turned to face the giant expanse of the women's section, pulsing under the fluorescents in electric color. This was obviously where the brand came alive. I breathed in the smell of fresh, commercial cotton. *Ahhhhh.* Intoxicating. I started making a tally in my head of all the items I'd pick up with my clothing allowance—my head spun with the abundance. I wanted it all!

Wrap dresses à la Furstenberg and Halston-esque jumpsuits hung from the face-outs, and glints of shiny metallic Lurex peeked from the swimsuit racks, Studio 54–chic. I detected the curation of Roz, filling the store with stylish homages to past fashion eras—the old, new look that made American Apparel pop.

The store decor was just as much of a spectacle. Covers of vintage porn mags with names like *Oui* and *Fox* tiled the walls, and shots of naked women on bicycles papered the cash wrap. A stack of *Vice* magazines waited for customers to grab with their purchase. Three small television sets stacked atop each other flickered through shots of a blonde wearing athletic socks and underwear, lounging on an overstuffed leather couch.

It was Natalie, the girl who was up to no good on the playground in the shots that lined the Factory walls. I recognized her instantly.

A tinkle of shop bells drew my attention to the door.

Two girls walked in—a Pamela Anderson blonde in Moon Boots and a little brunette in a Mötley Crüe tee and terry shorts with the waistband folded over.

"You're the new girl, right?" Moon Boots asked.

"Yep," I confessed. "I don't really know what I'm doing."

"Don't worry," the little one said. She had a face so young it looked like it belonged on a milk carton. "We'll help you."

III

In that first week, the work was easy, and the girls were nice.

Gia, the blonde, had giant cushiony lips that left wet spots on your cheek when she kissed you hello, and she was always kissing me hello. The other was Elyse, who had a modeling agent and an immigrant mom back in the Valley who counted on her to fulfill the first-generation American dream, Hollywood-style. She was nineteen years old but could pass for fifteen and often did at her numerous castings for TV commercials, which she'd dart out of the shop to hit almost every afternoon.

"You look great for your age," Elyse told me on that first day as we were stuffing duffel bags with newspaper and stacking them in a pyramid to display. "You're like, a really young twenty-three."

I had never met girls like these before. I was only a few years older than each of them, but they regarded me like a wise old sage, listening intently to my advice on everything from axing cheating boyfriends (I had left one behind in Philly) and easing menstrual cramps (masturbate to orgasm—it was foolproof). They were resolutely uninterested in politics, having only a rudimentary understanding of current events and even basic geography. Elyse once asked me if Canada was next to France.

I was finding them so refreshing after my aggressively intellectual college experience—sometimes it just felt good to be young and dumb with the girls. We'd check ourselves out incessantly in front of the dressing room mirrors, split twenty-five-cent cigarettes from the liquor store in the alley behind the shop on our fifteens, and keep each other informed of any celebrities who would wander in to sniff around, curious about this new brand that was starting to edge the pop-culture zeitgeist that spring.

I could always spot a celebrity right away. I identified Ryan Gosling as soon as he walked in the door with a motorcycle helmet under his arm. His smile glowed blue-white, the color of famous people's teeth—a dead giveaway. It was the summer after the release of *The Notebook*, and he came in to stock up on Summer Tees, a simple, white James Dean tee done over in sheer cotton with apple-red stitching along the seams.

Elyse was the one who pointed out Ashlee Simpson shopping for leggings five months after her *SNL* lip-syncing debacle, wearing her giant Chanel sunglasses indoors.

A few weeks after that, Queen Latifah asked to use the employee restroom.

The magical surrealism of Hollywood was infiltrating the store, and I got swept up in all of it. Handsome movie stars and feminist hip-hop legends shopped where I did, peed where I did. Beautiful girls on billboards were my friends. And in my first three months working there, I paid my bills and made rent every time. Barely. But still I was proud of myself—I was making things work here, building a new life, with Philly getting smaller and smaller in my rearview.

Before long, even Anarah warmed up to me. I started picking up all the little annoying responsibilities so that she could skip out whenever she needed—the paperwork, cash counting, stock refills. I'd wrangle the crew of backstock boys unloading boxes in the back room and delegate their tasks. I'd lock up the store every night, and Anarah would open it back up again in the mornings. We traded tasks like two mismatched bookends, holding the store together.

I had passed my test with flying colors.

"You know, at first I thought you might be another Dov girl," she said to me one afternoon as we were folding the raglans. "But you're really helping me out, here."

Dov girl.

That was the first time I heard that term. I asked Anarah what it meant.

"His girlfriends that are on the payroll," she said. "The girls in the ads, sometimes."

My mind went right to Ivy and her flirty smile on the billboard that hung over the shop. *Was Ivy a Dov girl*, I wondered?

Back then, the concept of an employee dating a boss didn't really ring any alarm bells for me. Back at Urban, even my boss, Beverly, lived with *her* supervisor—they had been in a relationship for years. Dating at work seemed sort of inevitable—you fall for people around you, and sometimes they're the people at work. And Dov was still young, nothing like Beverly's crusty old boss.

Anarah leaned under the cash wrap and rummaged around, pulling out an old copy of *Vice* with an American Apparel ad on the back.

In the shot, Natalie was leaning out of a car window, the rushing highway a blur around her. Her hand was stretched out, catching air, and her buttcheeks peeked out of a pair of cherry-red track shorts.

ROAD TRIP WITH AMERICAN APPAREL, the ad read.

The shot was taken from the driver's side. I had a sneaking suspicion who the photographer might be—the same man behind the wheel of the entire company.

"Natalie was the very first Dov girl," she said.

She explained that Natalie was the face of the brand in those early days, the girl in all the ads, always at Dov's side at the trade shows in Vegas. Natalie had once been his most reliable supporter and hardest worker, but right when things really started to catch on for the company, Natalie disappeared. She was missing for months, and no one knew where she went.

"But there was a hint," Anarah said, pointing to the photo.

I leaned in closer. At first glance, Natalie looked the same as she did in the shots at the Factory. Her hair was a little longer, she was thinner. But there was something off. I almost didn't notice it at first until Anarah pointed it out.

Something was up with Natalie's eyes. Her expression was empty, it didn't connect beyond the lens. Her pupils were huge, two black eclipses blotting out all the light. They reminded me of the cult girl's eyes at the mall.

Something wasn't right there.

Anarah explained that being a billboard girl had gone to Natalie's head.

"Too many nights partying on the Chateau Marmont rooftop."

Natalie would still come to work, but she would be useless, and after six months of spiraling—allowing plenty of other girls like Ivy and Roz to climb the ranks—Dov sent Natalie straight to rehab.

"He felt responsible for her downfall, in a way, so he had to take care of her," Anarah said. "But she's clean now—Dov bought her two French bulldog puppies to keep her sober."

I thought about Dov at the Factory, the garment workers cheering for him. I thought about Natalie, saved from the Hollywood abyss. Anarah told me that Dov even paid for the braces on her own teeth—a luxury unavailable to her, growing up with nothing in Van Nuys. Anarah once showed me a raised purple scar in the shape of a rectangle on her forearm where someone had heated up a Zippo and pressed it against her arm. She had a rough start and Dov was treating her now, giving her everything she had been missing, and making life better for her four-year-old daughter, too.

"I'm not a Dov girl," she told me defensively, although I hadn't asked. "Dov is so generous, he cares about all of us like that."

I remembered that Ivy had said the same thing, back at the Factory.

It was seeming truer every day. I wondered if I worked hard enough, what my reward would be. I wasn't interested in being a Dov girl—men beyond thirty may as well have been seventy-five to me, a hairy chest made me want to run for the hills—but being an American Apparel girl? I really wanted that, and I'd work as hard as I could to climb up and grab it.

III

One afternoon a delivery came for me at the shop. Anarah tossed a package across the cash wrap as I clocked in. It was a manila envelope, bulging in the middle and slightly war-torn from the voyage, my name written on it in Sharpie.

"This came from the Factory for you," Anarah said.

Ooh. What a thrill to receive something from the industrial utopia downtown, with my name on it.

"What is it?" I asked, tearing open the package. A new sample? Something to shoot on the roof with Ivy again?

"Dunno," Anarah said, leaning in. She was curious, too, and I detected a little envy. She never got special deliveries from the Factory.

I rustled through some tissue paper and turned it upside down.

My heart jumped into my throat as a few scraps of familiar-looking fabric tumbled out.

Oh no. It couldn't be . . .

A sad pile of felt was all that remained of what had once been my mom's glorious hat.

It had been sliced into pieces—the brim detached from the crown, which was now flat as a clock and defiled with slashes of white chalk.

It stared up at me, gruesome as Frankenstein's monster.

"Oh noo," Anarah said with a smirk. "You got spec'd."

Spec'd.

I knew the term already from Urban, shorthand for *fashion specification*—a garment taken apart to study its construction, so it can be turned into a pattern and mass-produced on the assembly line.

My beloved hat was no longer a hat—now it was just ingredients.

A deep, dark sadness settled over me. *Why hadn't Ivy warned me?* My mom's hat was special, and now it was ruined! What kind of evil trickery was that?

I stuffed it back into the envelope and put on a brave face for Anarah.

"It's just a hat," I said.

Still, I couldn't bear to throw the scraps away, even though they were useless to me now. I took them home, and later that night, I laid out the pieces and tried thinking critically about them.

My hat had been discovered, and soon it would be famous.

And in its sacrifice, I knew it would go on to achieve total fashion immortality. It would be manufactured in the Factory by happy workers, sold by happy retail employees, and make its way onto the heads of happy girls across the country. Those customers would go on to buy more American Apparel, who would in turn hire more fair-wage employees—an ouroboros of sustainability.

And besides, I couldn't get stuck on a piece of clothing. That was so selfish, so immature. I was a career woman now. The progress of the company was the most important, and I'd offer up anything of mine for its benefit. It was the least I could do for a company I believed in, run by a man who cares about his employees.

It was just a hat, after all.

III

One morning a few weeks later, I was awoken by a frantic call from Anarah at the shop. My shift wasn't supposed to start until the afternoon, but she needed me at the shop *now*.

"There's an emergency," she said, panic welling in her voice.

"We got bombed . . . *again*."

It was a hot morning in April, the start of LA's spring but already hotter than a Jersey Shore July. The heat wavered in silvery patches on the asphalt as I screeched the three blocks over, my mind whirling with questions.

Bombed?!

. . . Again??

I sped past the Sunset Foot Clinic sign, and my eye caught the spinning sign as the sad foot grimaced down at me. A bad omen. What would be waiting for me at the store? Anarah never let anyone see her sweat—especially me—so I knew from her reaction that it had to be something terrible. But when I arrived, it wasn't a pit of smoking rubble but a catastrophe of a different kind.

A PR disaster.

Every inch of the glass storefront was covered in wheatpasted flyers. The utility poles, the bus benches, even an innocent bystander of a scrawny tree—none were spared from the flyerbombing. Every last bit of open space at the corner of Alvarado and Sunset—that same intersection Dov had chosen because it was the busiest in all of LA—now it was completely papered over with flyers of his own face.

The flyers were budget-looking, printed off someone's home computer. But even through the pixelation, the muttonchops and the 1980s geek glasses were unmistakable.

The same man I had seen at the Factory was staring back at me.

Under his face, it said:

OBEY YOUR MASTER-BAITER.

I squinted, trying to decode the message.

MASTER-BAITER?

What did *that* mean? Was it a pun, or just an activist without a spell-check?

I stepped inside and locked the door behind me, the store eerily dark with all the paper filtering out the sunlight. I met Anarah in the employee bathroom where she was filling up a bucket of steaming water from the sink.

"We have to act quick," she said, breathing heavily. "We have to get these down *now*. This happened once before when the story came out, but I never thought it would happen again!"

The story? What kind of story could that be? I had so many questions I was dying to ask, but time was of the essence now—I had to move quickly to keep up with Anarah as we each took a handle on the bucket and lugged it outside.

The wheat paste had hardened overnight to the consistency of cement, and we heaved the hot water on the storefront to soften it up. Anarah had it down to a science, since she had done this before. She handed me a trowel, and as we got to work, she told me about the reporter and the article that had come out the previous summer in *Jane* magazine.

The story was called "Meet Your New Boss."

There had been a cute young reporter. "Dov's type," Anarah said.

In the few days that she had tailed him, eating meals with him, touring the Factory, hanging with his entourage, Dov had gotten a crush. And then he had gotten a little too comfortable.

"He ended up jerking off in front of her," Anarah said.

I dropped the trowel back in the bucket and stared at her.

Jerking off?

"I know how it sounds," Anarah said. "But she says in the article—he *asked* her if he could," Anarah said.

Oh. I guess that made things a little different?

"She came looking for a great story, and she got one. *Opportunist,*" Anarah said.

She started in on the next flyer, giving it a few angry scrapes.

That was the first time I had heard that word—"opportunist." It sounded vaguely victim-blamey to me, but was the reporter really a victim if she consented to watching? I could tell from Anarah's defensiveness what she thought—Dov was the real victim here, duped and used by a scoop-hungry reporter trying out some gonzo journalism to make a name for herself.

Anarah scrambled inside to answer a ringing phone, leaving me on the street to finish the rest. I wondered if the wheatpasters had been watching me last night, waiting for me to lock up and leave so they could get started. I wondered if they were watching me now, on my knees on Sunset Boulevard, scraping their handiwork off the glass.

I tried to reason with the uneasy voice in my head.

Dov was just being honest about sex, wasn't he? Wasn't that so much better than being some secret masturbating creep in the shadows? Here, the wolf wasn't wearing sheep's clothing, he was completely naked. And naked honesty was what the sex-positive revolution of the new millennium was all about, right? The sexual liberation of Gloria Steinem's era of feminism had turned into the sex positivity of ours, the birth control and miniskirts replaced with celebrity sex tapes and *Playboy* spreads. In this new era, a woman could own her own sexual appetite, make her own decisions.

OBEY YOUR MASTER-BAITER.

It was such an outdated interpretation of what was going on in the company, offensive in its basicness. American Apparel girls were our own masters here, no one was baiting us.

All it would take was one trip to the Factory for anyone to see that.

4
≡

The Dressing Room

The dust settled slowly in the aftermath of the flyerbombing, its effects lasting far into that summer of 2005. There was an opposition now, and they had come for us. *American Apparel versus the world!* The attack was like powerful adhesive that bound us all together, uniting the shop crew and drawing me even closer to the girls and Anarah. All my time on and off the clock was spent with employees of American Apparel—my new family.

I hadn't really had the chance to choose a side—I just found myself there, aligned with an eccentric, horny revolutionary because I worked for him. I had always been a rule follower and a good girl, but for the first time, a little taste of deviancy danced on my palate. It's a cliché for a reason—it felt good to be bad. Naughty-by-proxy. Dov's defiance of social norms was infectious, and once the news of my masturbating boss in *Jane* magazine mellowed a little, I started doubling down.

I began by wearing fewer articles of clothing to the shop. The styles I had been picking up with my clothing allowance in the spring—yoga pants and camis, stretchy pencil skirts with crop tops—were downright Amish compared to my summer looks—micro shorts no bigger than a pair of undies paired with bandeau bra tops. When Ivy would show up at the shop with a camera around her neck, I was right there with the other girls, shaking my ass for the camera.

An air of lawlessness began to spread through the store's routine operations. On Saturdays, we'd wear roller skates while we worked, sliding around the tiny shop like bumper cars on glass, one collision away from a lawsuit. Sometimes we'd drag a kiddie pool outside and splash around on Sunset in our bikinis to lure in potential customers, handing out Tecates indiscriminately, no checking of IDs. I discovered even the grainy shots of naked women on bicycles decorating the cash wrap were pirated from Queen's 1978 "Bicycle Race" music video, copyright laws be damned.

The words I heard Roz speak back at the Factory were turning into a company-wide motto: *This is American Apparel, we can do anything we want!*

And for a while, that delicious rebelliousness powered me along. But after a few weeks, the excitement died down and the reality of the job started to sink in. Maybe we were a revolution, but we were still a T-shirt shop, and after four months of holding it down for Anarah, I was getting antsy. Ivy had said all I had to do was prove myself at the shop and I'd move on to other things, but it seemed like my reliability had turned into a catch-22. I had made myself so useful that now I was stuck here, and working retail was slowly becoming a drag.

I was grateful for the steady paychecks, of course. With overtime I was making $575 a week before taxes, which would shake out to be about 28K a year—the exact salary I'd made at Urban. And thirty-two hours a week qualified me for employee health insurance, which had kicked in after my first ninety days. All the parent-pleasing perks of a real job were in my grasp, but not much of the personal satisfaction I'd envisioned my job would give me after that first trip to the Factory.

The brand was taking over LA storefronts—it seemed like every neighborhood had one in its proximity. One in Beverly Hills now, Westwood,

We-Ho, Studio City—I could barely keep track. The foot traffic in the store became heavier, the clientele needier. And I wasn't dealing with just hipsters and yoga moms and friendly celebs now; most of my day was spent picking up after garden-variety civilians in flip-flops who'd barge in, try on a mountain of clothes for fun, buy nothing, and leave the sweaty remains on the floor of the dressing room floor for me to pick up like I was their mother.

The last straw had been a simple mistake I had made on a customer's purchase one afternoon after Anarah left for the day. The store was crazy busy when a man in a two-tone bowling shirt approached the cash wrap to buy the new Tyvek zip-up jacket that had just come out that afternoon. When I first hung the array of crisp, white track jackets done over in the space-age polymer of Tyvek, I was pleased. Finally, the men's department was attempting to stay fashionably relevant and delve beyond basic hoodies and sweatpants. But Anarah told me the jackets only came about because Dov got a deal on a stockpile of the material from a house-insulation company and knew it would be a lucrative flip.

And he was right, the jackets were a hit. Limited styles like that would sell out in a few days, and the man buying one was lucky to get his hands on one. There was a long line stacking up behind him at the register, and in my hurry, I accidentally charged him twice for the jacket.

"Hold on, this'll just take a second," I said in my chirpy customer service voice. "Sorry for the inconvenience."

I smiled at him and the woman by his side as I clicked through the system to reverse the charge. I worked that register with the skill of a physician by that summer. It would only take a few seconds to issue his refund.

The man looked over at his companion and smiled a knowing smile. "Beauty and brains. They never go hand in hand," he said.

I was so surprised I dropped his card on the floor. As I bent behind the cash wrap, I let the sting of his insult absorb. I knew how ridiculous they were, but his words still managed to hurt me. I had never been called stupid before, and I wondered why this man felt so comfortable insulting me over an honest mistake.

Was it all the skin I was showing? The nearly naked women on the walls?

I would have loved to tell him that I found him just as stupid as his awful two-tone bowling shirt, but I didn't say a word. I gritted my teeth into a smile and continued serving him. My adolescence spent at crappy jobs for minimum wage had long taught me that working retail, waiting tables, making coffee—good customer service is the Lord's work. All walks of life and their bad behavior are greeted and treated with patience, tolerance, and humility because the job dictates it, and I considered that every time I tipped.

I was nearing the end of my rope. But when I was my most frustrated, spinning my wheels at the Sunset shop, dying for something to happen, is when I stumbled upon what would become my true purpose with the company. I never would have seen it coming—I figured that writing or styling or some kind of nerdly management is what I'd end up doing whenever I clawed my way to a position at the Factory.

Instead, what set me apart from the other girls and changed my course in the company, giving me the exciting life I had come to LA hunting for, was completely unforeseen. Like an asteroid hitting a planet and blasting it out of orbit, far into the depths of outer space—my career was about to take off into unchartered territories.

And it all happened in the dressing room.

III

"Can I try these on?" she asked.

I turned to see a teenage girl with a pair of the new thigh-high athletic tube socks in her hand, a tattered collection of music festival wristbands clinging to her wrist. She smiled at me shyly.

The socks were a brand-new style—a sexier, more modern take on the 1970s gym socks that had become American Apparel mainstays, but with the regulation white striping relocated to the thigh instead of calf. They came clipped to each other with a plastic tag tie, and I snipped them apart and handed them to her.

"So cute, right?"

"*So* cute," she said, and disappeared into the dressing room.

The shopgirls had started shifting a little, their presence thinning out on the floor—I was the only regular now. Anarah was busy with drop-offs and doctors' appointments for her kid, and Gia had started picking up hours at the Beverly Hills shop for a change of scenery. Elyse had moved to part-time as her modeling career began to flourish way down at the other end of Sunset Boulevard. It was getting lonely in the shop.

Occasionally, a teenaged merchandiser named Franc would pop in to help out, whipping our banal window displays into works of innovative genius—the same magic he'd work for Lady Gaga when he'd design her iconic meat dress for the 2010 MTV VMAs—but the fact was becoming apparent to me as I toiled, alone, in the busy shop.

We needed more girls on the floor.

So when the girl stepped out of the dressing room, twirling in front of the mirror in the new socks and a pleated mini, I saw an opportunity to help myself, and help her, too.

"Are you interested in a job?" I asked.

Her eyes lit up like I had handed her a golden ticket.

Her name was Dawn, a junior in high school with a few holiday retail seasons at Wet Seal under her belt and a peppy exuberance made for customer service.

"But I just started this week at the Gap," she said.

"The Gap?!" I asked. I screwed my face into a look of utter disgust. "This is not *the Gap*. This is a revolution!"

I had been looking for an opportunity to try out my own rough version of The Hustle—the impassioned stump speech that Ivy had drawn me in with that night at Little Joy—and I had found it in teenage Dawn, who wouldn't judge me if I couldn't quite pull it off yet.

I started by telling the story of my trip to the Factory, how I'd seen the workers cheering for Dov.

"He's a little unorthodox," I said, the *Jane* mag article flashing in my brain. "But that's our strength—doing things differently." I reminded her that the majority of what was sold at the Gap was made in sweat-shops overseas and saw her eyes widen sympathetically.

I told her this company was really run by a horde of business-savvy women—the same ones on the billboards outside. And most importantly—working for American Apparel was *fun*.

"You think you'll say that about the Gap?" I asked.

Dawn shook her head. She knew that one was true, and so did I. I'd spent one harrowing holiday season at GapKids during my sophomore year of high school and still hadn't recovered.

I told her about the clothing allowance, the celebrity visits, the roller skates on Saturdays. I assured her that this would be the best spot to spend those last few precious summers before college. I believed everything I told her, so I was very convincing.

She quit the Gap and started with us two days later.

When I lined Dawn up in front of the dressing room curtain to take her Polaroid—"Just a technicality," I said—I knew she would be a sure thing. Destined for Factory-approval.

Dawn looked like she'd stepped out of an American Apparel ad—a baby face with a curvy body, slightly bohemian, ethnically ambiguous. She was the definitive Classic Girl.

But I had no idea that hiring Dawn would be *my* golden ticket, too.

Everything would change for me with that one flash of the Polaroid.

III

The store phone had been ringing off the hook all afternoon.

"I want to meet Caralee," a man's voice would mumble. "How much?"

"She's not for sale, asshole!" Anarah would yell, slamming down the receiver.

The ad had debuted on the back of the *LA Weekly* that morning.

MEET CARALEE, it said at the top.

The Sunset shop's address and phone number were listed at the bottom, and we were getting inundated with calls from men who had mistaken it as an ad for an escort service.

In the shot, Caralee is arranged into a traditional cheesecake pose—on her back with her legs kicked up high and crossed at the ankles. The bottoms of her feet are blackened with floor grunge. Two golden crescents marbled with stretch marks peek from the edge of her hot shorts, and on one is a screaming red blemish.

I couldn't take my eyes off that zit—it's what made the ad work.

It was real and intimate, like a snapshot you'd take with your best girlfriends and hide in an old coffee can in the back of your closet when you're practicing the ropes of sexiness, just getting a feel for it. Caralee's expression is eager, wanting to please.

Anarah warned me I'd be fielding pervs on the phone for the rest of my shift and asked me to be sure to change out the floor mannequins before I left for the night. A headless woman, man, and little dog beckoned to me from atop their plexiglass display cubes.

Changing out the mannequins was my least favorite job of all the store duties. They were heavy, and expensive, as Anarah was always warning me. One slippery grip, and a fiberglass limb would bonk off the floor and spiderweb into cracks that she could spot as soon as she stepped inside. I figured I'd better get it over with now while the store was slow.

I had just skinned last week's looks off them and was taking a breather when the door chimes rang out and in walked a girl I was *sure* I recognized.

She looked so familiar, but from where? Was she an actress? Or a girl from back home?

When she lowered her big brown shield shades, I saw her face, and I recognized that expression. Friendly and eager.

I looked down at the MEET CARALEE ad, still sitting on the cash wrap, and then back at the girl.

A-ha!

Caralee must have been conjured here by some kind of horny witchcraft—all those men who had been calling all morning looking for her had summoned her, and she appeared.

As I got ready to introduce myself—I didn't have to say I was the new girl anymore after Dawn's addition, at least—the iPod's shuffle function rolled into a song from the *Boogie Nights* soundtrack, which stopped Caralee dead in her tracks. It was a groovy instrumental number—amorphous Latin soul with a woman moaning and panting over maracas.

"I love this song!" she squealed, and broke into a series of humping motions, meted out in time with the music. This wasn't like any dancing I had ever done, all that self-conscious bopping with the girls back in the dorm. Caralee was grinding to the tune simply because she had caught the beat and rode it across the floor. She didn't care who was watching.

I checked her out while she danced. She was curvy as a Botticelli painting, with giant breasts straining her white tee and an inch of soft belly edging out from the hem. She had dark hair and big brown eyes, and smelled like soap and minty toothpaste when she hugged me hello. She giggled like a freak when I introduced myself, though I hadn't said anything particularly funny. But it got me giggling, too.

Caralee was a strange Hollywood amalgam—Marilyn Monroe mixed with Anna Faris.

I liked her instantly.

"Anarah said you were short on girls today, so I thought I'd swing by," she said, taking a mannequin limb from my hand. I hadn't even realized I was still holding it.

"These guys are easier with two people, for sure," she said.

We got down to work, and as Caralee helped me with the mannequins, her hands deftly clicking the joints into place, my name finally clicked with her.

"You're the one!" she yelled. "I was at the Factory when the Polaroid of the new Sunset girl came in. Dov was shaking it in everyone's face, saying the girl was perfect. He was asking everyone who you were."

Dov wanted to know who I was? I felt a thrill zip through me.

"He thinks you have vision," Caralee said.

I hadn't seen Dov since that first day at the Factory. Hearing he approved of my hiring of Dawn was like a faint grumble from Olympus that the gods were pleased.

Dov thought I had *vision*? They were talking about *me* at the Factory?

Finally I was getting noticed, and all I had done was hire a pretty girl! Imagine what I could really get around to accomplishing for the company when I tried.

As we finished up the mannequins, I was flying high. I starting dancing along with Caralee, too, groping the male mannequin's crotch to make her laugh. When I told her about the calls we had been getting at the store, she dissolved into laughter.

"It's just been that kind of day," she told me, sighing. "You won't believe the morning I had."

Caralee had treated herself to an expensive massage in Thai Town to celebrate her *LA Weekly* ad, and was surprised to find a sexy Brazilian masseur waiting for her behind the curtain.

"He had giant hands," she said. "Right away, I was turned on."

I imagined Caralee and the masseur in the dimly lit room smelling of eucalyptus. Caralee, slick with oil and perspiration, under a huge set of Brazilian hands.

Caralee told me all it took was a few suggestive moans—a nudge here, a grind there—and the massage turned into something different altogether. It had concluded in a happy ending.

Caralee's happy ending.

"He went down on me," she exclaimed, in earshot of a couple customers. They turned to stare.

"I couldn't help it," she said, shrugging. "He got me so hot."

I stared at her as I tried to process this information. The concept of getting head from a random stranger you paid for a service wasn't even in my realm of possibility that summer. But Caralee told me the story as casually as one might recommend a dentist.

"You should try him out," she advised.

I had so many questions but started with the one I was most curious about.

"Did you tip?" I asked.

"Of course. I'd never stiff a service worker on his tip."

I had never met a girl who talked about sex like this. It flew in the face of the time-honored boundaries usually painted around the act. When it should happen, and with whom, and under which circumstances.

When Madonna had French-kissed Britney Spears at the VMAs a couple of summers ago, everyone had lost their minds. But I knew that was all just an act—performative sexuality aimed for an audience of the male gaze. Nothing new there. But here was Caralee, getting off how she wanted and when she wanted. Tossing the "sacredness" of sex to the wind and going for it.

My sexual résumé cited hundreds of uninspired hours of missionary sex with my ex, but Caralee's sexual appetite was voracious—a real thing. At Bryn Mawr I had studied sexual liberation, but girls like Caralee were actually living it. Her activities with the masseur weren't even in the same solar system as my experiences, and it was starting to make me feel as self-conscious as a virgin. I had a lot of catching up to do.

There and then I decided I would be friends with her, and I would try to be like her—the archetypal cool girl breezing through her wild, sexy life.

III

When night crept in and the store was quiet, Caralee disappeared. I didn't think anything of it. There was nothing unusual about someone getting lost on the clock at the shop. Retail is a boring mistress, and there were many creative ways to make your shift move along faster. The counter at Burrito King next door served up scalding little taquitos in tomatillo salsa, two for a dollar. Plenty of cute backstock boys to chat with in the stockroom. I figured Caralee was up to one of those activities.

The store was empty, like it usually was right before close. I was sure because I had just executed a final sweep of the dressing room and found it empty. I gathered a few stray hangers, tucked the curtains back behind their hooks, and settled in at the cash wrap to scroll Perez.

There was Lindsay, clutching a bottle of VOSS, looking dazed in the paparazzi lightning. She was really transitioning into a regular party-monster these days, her star just starting to tarnish from too much exposure to limelight. Oh no, what was she doing out until dawn with *Jared Leto*? No good was going to come of that.

Suddenly a movement from the dressing room area broke my concentration.

I was sure it had been empty a few moments ago, but now it was definitely occupied. The curtains were swaying from some sort of rhythmic movement inside. I figured a customer must have snuck in without me knowing, so I headed over to check in and see if they needed any other sizes. The dressing room curtains weren't closed all the way—they were slightly ajar in the middle. And in that tiny sliver of space, I saw two people engaged in some kind of sexual frenzy. They were pressed against each other, hands everywhere, going at it like two wild monkeys in heat, slurping and grunting.

What the hell was going on in there?

If I weren't so surprised, I would have laughed. I had stumbled onto a performance of passion that was as try-hard as a soft-core porn on cable after dark, like bad acting.

What had gotten into these customers? Who would be crazy enough to make out in the dressing room, of all places? It was dusty and dank, and I knew it hadn't been vacuumed in weeks because I was supposed to be the one doing it. How was I going to get them to *stop* so I could close the store?

A pair of dark eyes shot out and caught mine.

"Somebody's watchin' me," a man's voice said.

It was high and thin, with a nasal quality to it. A voice from that day at the Factory.

Oh no.

I felt all the blood rush to my face as the curtains flew open.

There he was. Wearing a beige terry cloth polo unbuttoned all the way, a few dark scraggles of chest hair escaping his collar. A pair of nearly see-through nylon joggers rose in a tent just below his waistband.

It was Dov. The great Orwellian eye was standing in front of me, in the flesh.

"I'm sorry," I sputtered, my face starting to blaze with embarrassment. "I thought you were a customer. I thought you were trying something on."

He snorted with laughter and jerked his thumb back in the direction of the dressing room.

"I was *about* to," he said.

Out of the dressing room stepped Caralee. She smiled sheepishly at me, the smile of someone who had gotten caught.

"I'm sorry," I told her. "I'm so sorry!"

I would have stood there apologizing all night, but Dov cut me off. He held up a hand and commanded me to silence.

"It's okay. You don't have to apologize. Who wouldn't want to watch two people getting it on?"

Oh my god.

That wasn't what had happened at all! My face was on fire—this was *not* how I wanted to meet my new boss.

We stood eye to eye in front of the dressing room. I noticed he was only an inch or two taller than I was—he had seemed so much bigger that day at the Factory. His stare slid over my body like a hand, and when it returned to my eyes, I noticed it had come back somewhat disinterested.

I was relieved but also surprised to find that I was a little disappointed. He knew right away that I wasn't a Caralee.

I shifted uncomfortably under his gaze, wishing I had worn a better outfit, or at least brushed out my greasy bun this morning. *Fuck!* I was really blowing it.

Caralee cut the awkward silence with an introduction.

"Dov, this is Kate. She's the one who scouted Dawn."

The mention of Dawn broke Dov free from his inspection of me. He threw his hands in the air like he had made a great discovery.

"*You're* the one," he said. "Let me tell you why I liked that girl you found, why I noticed *her* above all the rest. Here's this girl, you see her."

He cut a square in the air with his hands and then wiggled his fingers in it.

"She's cute, but she's not trying too hard. She's no beauty queen, but she's definitely hot. She's *fuckable*, you know? Can you find me more girls just like that?"

I opened my mouth to say something, but he kept right on talking.

"People are always sending me Polaroids of model material, girls in mesh thinking they're hot shit—I don't want that. Listen, I need you in New York this weekend. I've got three shops there that need your vision. Go scout for girls."

Go to New York this weekend?

Questions started flooding my brain. How would I get my plane tickets? Where would I stay? Would I just wander the city, searching for the fuckable?

Just go to New York and *scout*? What did that even mean?

I didn't get the chance to ask any questions. Dov's cell phone started vibrating in his holster, and he bolted for the exit.

"Gotta take this," he tossed over his shoulder. I heard the chimes twinkle serenely as he rocketed out the door, Caralee tailing behind him. "And clean that filthy dressing room!" he yelled back at me.

I was alone on the floor again, my heartbeat pumping in my ears. Everything seemed brighter around me, more vivid. I could hear the fluorescents buzzing in their tracks above me, the traffic honking outside. What the hell had just happened in here?

Ivy called from the Factory just a few minutes later.

"I've got your cards all printed up," she said. "And I bought you a one-way ticket to JFK."

"One-way?" I asked. "How long will I be there?"

"Until the work is done," Ivy said. "There's a company apartment over the shop, you'll stay there."

A company apartment? My head spun with more questions, but I started with the most important question of all.

"But how will I get paid?" I couldn't just jet off to New York. Rent was due next week.

"Just email me your hours, you won't be stamping a time card anymore," she said. "You can make your own schedule now."

No more time cards? My *own* schedule? I wanted to explode with joy. Everything Ivy had told me the night at Little Joy was coming true like a premonition—I shouldn't have doubted her.

An hour later, a messenger delivered the cards.

I tugged one from its rubber-banded bundle—the same scouting card Ivy had handed me when we met, but with my own name and info at the bottom. It was official.

I was a real-deal American Apparel girl now.

I tucked the cards into my bag, lovingly. I had heard about men in suits climbing the corporate ladder quickly, but nothing quite like this. Maybe the glass ceiling was the last century's problem, or were the rules just different at American Apparel? It was beginning to seem like there were none. I felt wild and totally free and totally unleashed, an animal freed from a trap—New York first, then who knows?

As I headed home, a little bit of Bryn Mawr started whispering questions in my ear. Was seeing the company CEO making out with a shopgirl normal? Definitely not, not on its surface anyway. But nothing about this company was normal, that was why it was working so well, right? And besides, just like the journalist, Caralee had clearly been game. How could I fault her for what she wanted? She was a grown woman, old enough to make her own choices and sleep with anyone she pleased, whether it be her boss or her sexy Brazilian masseur.

As I drove back to my apartment that night, I was really feeling myself. This was where my journey was going to start. I could hear all Seven of the Sisters blazing their trumpets along my way home—look, they said. There goes a good one, a smart one. Playing the game, but still a hard worker about to set off on her own adventure.

There goes a real modern woman, they said.

5

The Party

Caralee called me the next afternoon while I was packing for New York.

I considered apologizing for walking in on her in the dressing room, but she didn't mention it, so neither did I. I got the feeling that Caralee's personal life was so rich in sexual adventure, it wasn't a big deal to her to have someone stumble into it from time to time.

"Wanna hang?" she asked.

I was practically giddy, desperate to get a hang in the books with my intriguing new friend. There was so much to learn from her. But my flight was scheduled for early the next morning, and I still had so much to do! I had no idea what to pack beyond my scouting cards, a toothbrush, and a bag full of American Apparel clothes. Would I be staying until the weather got cold? It was only August, but I knew how September lurked on the East Coast, waiting to ambush summer overnight. Did I need a heavy coat? I had given mine away when I moved, hoping I'd never need it again.

So much of my trip was unknown, which didn't help the roiling case of airport anxiety that was building up in me, like it always does the day before a big trip. When I flew out of Philly for the last time, I had been in such a nervous state I left my tickets behind, and the yellow cab had to double back around for them. Then I was late to the airport, late through the security line, and late to the gate, where I was the last person to board. By the time I collapsed into my seat in coach, my throat was closed up so tight I could barely drink my complimentary ginger ale, and all the exhilaration I thought I'd feel moving across the country was replaced by numb exhaustion. But this time I wanted everything to be perfect, and I needed as much time as possible to coax myself into a Zen-like state for the stressful voyage.

Caralee laughed when I told her I needed to pack.

"But you don't leave until *tomorrow morning*," she said. "There's plenty of time, and whatever you don't bring, you can expense on the road."

Expense on the road? This was a fascinating development. Caralee told me any money I'd spend would be reimbursed as soon as I got back.

"Save your receipts," she said.

I was barely scraping by on my weekly paychecks, but it dawned on me that was all going to change once I was traveling for the brand. All my meals, my clothes, my travel expenses—American Apparel would be footing the bill now. My new scouting job was going to lead directly to more money in my pocket, and Caralee could hear my excitement burbling through the phone.

"Screw packing—let's have a party," she said. "To celebrate."

She said she'd invite the Sunset girls, and we'd take some pictures in some samples from the Factory. The party would be a two-birds-one-stone kind of deal—a celebration in honor of my new promotion *and* a photoshoot for the company that we could expense.

"What do you think?" she asked.

A late-night party before an early flight was making my airport anxiety spike already. But how could I say no to Caralee? She wanted to throw me a party, which was making me feel very special. I knew she lived in a company apartment in Echo Park—Dov started renting out apartments in the cities where the brand was taking root, a way to save on hotel expenses and a homier place for the traveling girls to stay. Cara-lee lived in one full-time, and I was anxious to see what the vibe was like before I arrived in New York and moved into one myself.

I imagined the company apartments would be full of billboard girls, living harmoniously in a modern loft full of modern Togo couches and swinging macramé. But when I asked if we'd be throwing the bash there, Caralee groaned.

"The San Fran girls have taken it over!" she said. They had come down last week for training and were posted up in there, turning it into a noxious hotbox of smoldering palo santo and Blue Dream.

"Can we have it at your place instead?" she asked.

My roommate was out of town for the weekend, and I had the apart-ment to myself. Maybe I could even squeeze a little packing in—killing two birds with one stone myself. It would only be us and the Sunset girls. Sounded kind of tame as far as parties went. How wild could things get?

"Sure," I told her.

"I'll pick you up in ten minutes," Caralee said. "We'll need supplies."

III

An hour later, I was roaming the shops on Vermont Ave. with the girls. After Caralee and I picked up Gia at her place and two bottles of rum at Bogie's Liquor, we made our way up Sunset to Los Feliz for a little shop-ping expedition of our own.

Gia and Caralee were in a bouncy mood, and so was I. A fun evening and a photoshoot awaited, and we were all delighted to be in a retail environment where we could serve ourselves, for once. We had all just shared a bag of tamales, and I embarrassed myself when I pulled out the first one and tried to eat the husk. Gia burst out laughing, but Caralee didn't make me feel dumb about it at all.

"The same thing happened to me when I moved here," she said, nodding solemnly. I felt our new friendship grow another inch. I was like a wilted houseplant who had found a way to stretch toward some long-denied sun.

We passed by Y Que, a string of yellowing FREE WINONA shirts baking in its sunny window, and headed to Squaresville to clack through their racks of musty vintage. I was spinning through a carousel of sunglasses on the cash wrap when I heard Caralee's phone ring.

I surveyed the rows of candy-colored Lolita shades with heart-shaped lenses and tried on a purple pair. I peered up at the mirror to see if they worked—I'd always wanted a pair, but they had never seemed quite right on me. But my style was changing in LA, I was becoming more adventurous. I could probably pull them off now. When I turned back to the girls to get their opinion, they were distracted.

Gia and Caralee were swapping the phone—a grenade-shaped Nextel—back and forth, the antenna wobbling. Their voices were low. They were completely immersed in the call—they didn't notice or care that I stood by, listening in. I had all but vanished to them. The call was the only thing in their world at that moment.

Gia was talking in a babyish voice I had never heard her speak in before.

"*Mmmm.*" She sighed. "I guess so."

She passed the phone back to Caralee, whose boisterous cheerleader voice I'd been hearing all afternoon had turned silken as a 1-900 operator.

"Sounds good to me," Caralee purred.

Who were these girls talking to?

"Bye, Daddy," Caralee said. She handed the phone back to Gia.

"Bye, Daddy."

In that moment, I knew exactly who was on the other end of that line. It was definitely not Caralee's father back in Springfield. I had heard the rumors about Dov's familial nickname, but this was the first time I ever experienced it in action.

As I bought my sunglasses, I heard Caralee and Gia talking to each other about the new American Apparel store opening in Berlin, and everything started to click into place. *Berlin!* Glamorous, sullen city of black turtlenecks and industrial music. It seemed to be the antithesis of LA—of course, all the girls were clamoring to go. But it seemed like Caralee and Gia had figured out their own way to get there.

I didn't say anything on the car ride home, even though I was pretty sure I knew it all.

I slouched low in the backseat of Caralee's car, wearing my new sunglasses, even though the sun was starting to dip.

My first instinct was to pass judgment on them. *I* didn't need to sleep with Dov to move up in the company. Look how I just scored a trip to New York simply because I had dedicated myself and found a springboard out. *That* was how you earn rewards—didn't these girls know? I was here to work, to climb to the top with only my own ambition giving me a boost, and that's how I'd make my way to New York, Berlin, and beyond.

Then I felt a little ashamed for being so judgmental about my new sex-positive friends, so I tried turning to feminist reason. Maybe using their sexuality to get a free trip to Berlin was actually the most feminist thing of all. Maybe Caralee and Gia were actually using Dov to get ahead, not the other way around.

And if that were the case—then why wasn't I included? I was the best feminist around, goddamnit! A tiny bit of jealousy burned like acid inside me. I couldn't ignore the awful feeling of being left out, even though the last thing I wanted was to have sex with Dov. I still wanted him to want me—I couldn't help it. What made me so different from the others that I hadn't even been considered?

I knew why he wanted Caralee, but Gia was like me—skinny, exotic as a Saltine, not really Dov's type at all. It must be all that long blond hair, I figured.

No, there had to be something else about me—beyond my physicality—that was setting me apart from the girls. Something Dov sussed out as soon as he met me in that dressing room. It was as if he knew instantly that I was nothing but a sexually inexperienced, tamale husk–eating good girl, and not the type who'd have a threesome with Caralee for tickets to Berlin.

He could tell right away I was not a real American Apparel girl. And I was going to have to do something about that.

III

Caralee was in charge of making drinks for the party that night.

Mojitos—a cocktail I'd never had before. She had brought along a blender from the company apartment and was mixing up the first batch of the evening in my tiny kitchen.

First a long pour of rum went in over the ice, setting it crackling. Then a whole bouquet of mint, stems and all. She squeezed in a gloop of indigo-colored syrup from a plastic bottle with a cactus on the label.

"Agave, to make them sweet," she shouted over the grind of the blender.

I had never heard of agave before but nodded anyway. After my tamale experience, I figured I'd better keep my mouth shut. She poured the concoction into my glass and topped it off with a fizzle of Topo Chico.

I took a sip.

It tasted grassy and sweet and pleasant going down. She had been generous with the rum—only a few sips in, and a lovely warmth was spreading from the top of my forehead and trickling down my spine, making my body feel loose and easy as a drip of warm sap.

"Good?" Caralee asked.

"Terrific," I said, draining the rest of the glass. "I'll have another."

Forty-five minutes and two mojitos later, the bathroom door opened and Caralee stepped out. She had changed into a cami and matching hipster underwear in Clementine—a new red-orange color that buzzed off her tan skin like neon. My eyes wandered to her crotch, where a curious blue orb of light was glowing through the cotton.

"What *is* that?" I asked.

Caralee reached in her underwear and extricated a glowing plastic ice cube.

"The cigarette girls were handing them out at Cinespace."

She fiddled with the cube—a battery-operated doodad to make your drink glow Parliament blue—and it switched over from a static glow to a pulsing twinkle.

"That's more like it," she said, placing it back in her underwear. We both started laughing.

"Don't worry," she said. "I got one for everyone."

Each of us changed into the panty sets in my bedroom. Gia's in Baby Blue, Elyse's in Shamrock Green, and mine in Mustard, the last choice. Then Caralee handed each of us an electric ice cube, and once each of our crotches were fully a-twinkle, she shepherded us into the bathroom, carrying a digital camera she had borrowed from the Factory.

Caralee was clearly the most experienced with American Apparel shoots, so we deferred to her expertise. She thought we should be wet in the cami sets. The cotton would melt away to nothing, but in a technical sense, we would still be wearing the brand in the shots.

I was happy to oblige—the first one in the shower. I feel light and free as a feather in the warm spray, and not a bit self-conscious at all. I mug for the camera, feeling myself. Stretching my now-transparent cami over my chest so Caralee can get a really good shot. I'm not sure what's gotten into me—maybe the agave?

Then Gia hops in next to me, and soon she's all wet and transparent, too. We give model face, we laugh, we throw our arms around each other. Soon we run out of ideas, and before I even know what's happening, her giant pair of lips is coming for mine, and then we're kissing.

Snap snap snap. Caralee clicked away.

Of course I had kissed girls before. An egalitarian game of spin the bottle in high school, once on Ecstasy at an electroclash night in Philly. And I knew by then that kissing your girlfriends was a highly effective way to be sexy and rebellious. The safest way to interact with the male gaze, a kind of easy-come sexy currency you always had in your back pocket. Why not?

Gia kissing me was the least she could do after I had been so rudely passed over at Squaresville. And I was comfortable kissing her. Just a few days earlier she had tucked in my tampon string after it had snuck out of my bikini bottoms during an afternoon sunbathing on the roof of her apartment. I had never experienced such exquisite closeness with girls before.

Up until then, Bryn Mawr had felt like the only place I'd ever really belonged. But this new species of untamed girls? They were starting to feel like home to me.

Snap snap snap.

Elyse, the shy one, had taken over photographer duties. I could tell the kissing made her a little uncomfortable. She was Catholic and once told me she had learned that a lady's armpit was a private part. I had been raised Catholic, too, but luckily no one was a freak about it. I couldn't help but feel a little thrill in outsexying her—I had no hang-ups like that. I was down for anything, a Girl Gone Wild.

Caralee jumped in the tub, and we all lay down in there together. We barely fit, the three of us squeezing on top of each other, a mass of slippery limbs and translucent underwear and blinking ice cubes. I saw that Caralee's tank top had ridden up, and the low globe of her bare breast was peeking out from the bottom of the hem. I reached for it.

And then Caralee was kissing me, too. Pleasant, comfortable girl kisses. The tub was hard under my back, but the girls were soft all around me. The camera clicked away, and I thought about Squaresville and how I was going to prove them all wrong.

I was one of these girls—*an American Apparel girl*. The most sex-positive of them all! I was going to make them see. And Dov? I would make him see, too. I would work the hardest and be the sexiest one who would never have sex with him.

I would do it the right way.

III

I woke the next morning to the SuperShuttle guy pounding on my door. *FUCK!*

Not again! I couldn't miss this flight, not my very first scouting trip. It would be so humiliating explaining to Ivy—or worse, to Dov—that I had been irresponsible and overslept.

When exactly had we gone to bed? I tried to dredge up the rest of the night but came up with vapors. Caralee was snoring peacefully beside me in bed. When had the other girls left? How had they gotten home? What happened after my third Mojito?

The driver hauled my duffel out the door with an annoyed grunt as I ran amok in my apartment, shouting apologies and gathering the last-minute ephemera I would need for the trip. I grabbed my stack of scouting cards—couldn't forget those—my iPod, its tangle of headphones. Most importantly, my plane ticket—nonstop coach from LAX to JFK. I folded it and stuck it in my bra like I had seen women do with precious objects.

God, my head was pounding. My throat felt like it was lined in gauze, and my stomach was a seesaw with two terrible options lurking at either end. I ran to the bathroom to gather my toothbrush and took a long, pathetic slurp out of the sink's faucet. A handful of blinking ice cubes lit up in a few inches of murky water at the bottom of the tub, mementos from the night before.

I was beginning to remember.

The girls, the kissing.

The pictures.

Ughhh. In the moment, it had felt so freeing, the true embodiment of harmless, sexy fun. But now I imaged the pictures finding a home in that mysterious database back at the Factory. What would become of them when they got out of our hands? Who would see them? How would I look to someone who hadn't been to the party?

The SuperShuttle driver angrily tooted his horn outside. I winced and zipped up my backpack.

"Caralee. Lock up for me!" I yelled.

"*Mmmm-hmm.*"

Caralee smiled sleepily with her eyes closed and rolled over.

I settled into the carpeted cocoon of the minivan, and the window was smooth and cool against my pounding head. And just as I was drifting off, I started thinking about another weird party I threw, back at the dorms.

It was another time where I had thought I was so grown up, evoking the same kind of revolutionary girl power that was pulsing through the party last night. We were acting like men, weren't we? We were the ones in charge here. We didn't feed anybody's sexual appetite but our own. But I should have learned that first time that things can't flip around quite so easily. How could I have forgotten?

It was my nineteenth birthday, and I was determined to find the best-looking stripper available.

I had just learned about the male gaze in a gender studies class, and I was thinking it would be an interesting experiment—a feminist rite, actually—to hire a man to strip down and dance in front of me and my classmates for my birthday party. We'd be flipping that male gaze right on its head. We'd turn it into something even better—the *female* gaze, a hallmark of the millennium, I was sure. It was February of 2000, and it gleamed all around us with its shiny veneer of newness.

But I was finding it very difficult to find the right man to objectify.

I was scrolling through a glitchy GeoCities site for a company called Hunk-O-Mania, sorting through their selection of flexing men, determined to pick out the best-looking one. Most of them were ugly as toads, eyes and muscles bulging. *Blechh.* They were all too masculine, caricatures of the ideal male form that were such a turnoff to my teenage brain. No one appealed to me.

But right when I was about to give up, a handsome, boyish face started sharpening through the pixels. He had gentle eyes, pouty lips, a flow of romantic ringlets. A slim build, a hairless chest. I noticed he was wearing one gold hoop earring and a three-cornered hat with a skull and crossbones on it.

STINGRAY THE PIRATE—$150/45 minutes, cash.

Perfect!

I called Hunk-O-Mania and told them I had my man. I signed out the dorm's lounge for the night—the one with the imposing stone fireplace and the baby grand piano. A fitting setting to match the gravity of the momentous event that was about to take place, I knew.

Up until that point, I had no idea what hiring an exotic dancer would really entail. I had a hazy vision of tossing dollars at a man who would jump from a cake and strut around in front of us as he stripped down to nothing but a smile. What an absolute feminist fantasy! I'd be flipping around that patriarchal power structure of the last century with one simple, yet revolutionary, act. Gender was just a construct anyway, and it was time to do a little deconstructing.

As I looked at the excited faces of my hallmates that evening, I detected a sort of admiration in their eyes. This was going to be an experience we'd remember for the rest of our lives! *The night we reclaimed the female gaze.* The best part was that it had all been my idea. Perhaps I'd return for our twentieth reunion to find the dorm renamed in my honor—this was important stuff we were doing here.

I was ready.

The only problem was that Stingray was running late. A winter snowstorm had blown in, icing out the roads and having the same effect on my party. Just as the girls were starting to make noises about heading back to their rooms to study, a police officer walked in.

"Is there a party here tonight?" he asked.

The room went silent with fear.

He walked over to me. "Is this your party?"

I looked around at the world's tamest party and was suddenly struck with the panic that I had broken the rules, and now I would be punished. Maybe booking an exotic dancer in the dorm lounge had been going too far. Could I get expelled for this?

I felt the other girls watching me, seeing how I'd react.

"Yes," I said, bravely. "It's my birthday."

The police officer did the very last thing I'd expect a police officer to do.

He picked me up and lifted me to his shoulders. Not the way you usually sit on someone's shoulders, with everyone facing the same direction. I was turned the other way around, so the policeman's mouth was an inch from the zipper of my Miss Sixtys.

I heard all the girls gasp, and then it dawned on me.

Stingray!

But somehow the romantic pirate I had picked out on the internet had been replaced with a bodybuilding Jersey guido with frosted tips. This was *not* the hunk I ordered.

"Are you Stingray?" I demanded.

But Stingray ignored my questions, instead flipping me upside down, my knees hooked to his shoulders like an aerialist at the circus. From this vantage point, I could see my classmates' expressions turn from amused grins to horrified Os as it dawned on them exactly what the next forty-five minutes of their life was going to involve.

It turns out male strippers don't just flex and strip while you watch from afar, like I had imagined—what they *actually* do is pick you up and go through the motions of fucking your brains out. Stingray had my legs flossed around his midsection, gyrating against me so violently that my molars were starting to rattle.

Oh God! This was not how this was supposed to go at all.

Stingray switched gears and slowly lowered me into a chair. I covered my eyes and heard a whisper of Velcro, and when I opened them, his cop costume had disappeared and a Day-Glo orange G-string waggled a few inches from my forehead.

He turned his attention to the other girls in the room.

Stingray was a power-humper—his routine was more like an athletic exhibition than any sort of display of sexuality. I noticed that his bare knees were bleeding from the tug of the polished floor as he hurtled himself at each of us.

One by one the girls abandoned the lounge and fled for the safety of their rooms, leaving only me, determined to see this through to the end. Running away like the rest of them would be like admitting the truth to myself—I had obviously made a terrible miscalculation.

My experiment had failed. I had tried to behave like a man, and it backfired. It turns out that the male gaze is too strong to appropriate. Even when you try to take command, it wants to return to its natural state, like a domesticated wolf. I had no choice but to let go and submit to Stingray. He smiled down at me and held me tightly against him, humping my lights out.

I looked at my watch. I had forty-one minutes left to go.

Stingray had stripped down all right, but he revealed an embarrassed, gullible girl who had gotten in way over her head, and not a sexual revolutionary who was blasting a hole through the interminable landscape of the patriarchy. I should have known that you can't just switch things around that easily.

But that wasn't what had happened at the photoshoot party last night, right? There hadn't even been a single man there—this was all for us. I had been trying to bury the memory of Stingray and the whole mortifying experience for years, so why was he popping up now? I was on my way to New York City, about to start a new adventure. I should be feeling my most confident.

I pushed the stripper from my mind.

It was my time to shine now.

6

The Window

My bedroom in the New York company apartment looked just like the background of an American Apparel ad. The feather duvet covering the bed—which was just a mattress and a box spring stacked on the floor—was tousled in a way that made me think the last occupant had rolled out of it minutes before. A row of minimal glass shelves were shoved against the wall, empty except for a lighter and someone else's toothbrush. There was a lone CD jewel case—*The Emancipation of Mimi*—with nothing inside.

Above the bed, an arrangement of fifteen vintage *Hustler* cover girls greeted me. One of them—Miss March 1976—had her denim coochie cutters spread so wide it looked like she was preparing to give birth. I tallied up the years—thirty, *wow!*—since she shot this cover. Miss March would be fifty, maybe fifty-five now. I couldn't see her face, it was cropped out of frame.

She was wearing a bandeau top that was valiantly trying to contain a giant set of breasts, and she was also wearing knee-high athletic socks—white with red and blue striping—identical to the ones we were selling that summer. Another cover girl had on a silver lamé bikini.

A-ha.

So that's where they came from. The socks, the running shorts, the swimsuits, even my mom's floppy hat—all forms of fashion plagiarism. Most of American Apparel's new styles were just recycled garments from the 1970s, the era when Dov's libido came of age. Even these magazines were no doubt from his own personal stash, doubling as high art here in the company apartment, four floors above the Lower East Side store.

I was out of breath from the hike up the stairwell. A girl named Shuli, the store manager, walked me upstairs and showed me around the tiny apartment. It wasn't much—nothing like I had imagined. Just a few tiny bedrooms, a galley kitchen, a bathroom so compact you could smoke in the tub and ash in the toilet.

"Call me if you need anything," Shuli said. "Weed guy comes on Thursdays."

She was wearing Robin Hood boots and the stretch pencil mini over a pair of leggings—something that never occurred to me to put together. It was either one or the other, never both. The girls here didn't show the same kind of skin that we did in the shops in California. I figured that must be out of necessity—protecting their extremities from all that forensic material on the subway seats, the rats leaping from trash cans. The eyes and hands of urban perverts were probably more active in a city like this one. Nothing like Los Angeles, where we stayed untouchable in our cars.

Shuli's whole outfit made her seem impenetrable and strong, like urban armor. She wasn't particularly friendly, but I figured that was probably a New York thing, too. I couldn't help but wonder if she was a Dov girl, and I could tell by the way she was looking at me that she was wondering the same thing.

As she turned to the door, I realized she had never given me a key.

"No keys, unfortunately," she said. "All the girls kept leaving town with them."

She reached into her waistband and pulled out an American Apparel gift card.

"Just jimmy the lock with this," she said, handing it to me. "Works like a charm."

And then she was gone, and it was just me and the *Hustler* girls and a window full of New York City outside, waiting to cover me like seductive black velvet. Tomorrow I would start my first day of scouting out there.

I felt anticipation rise in me like a wave.

This was the New York I had always wanted.

I don't mean to sound like a New York virgin—because I grew up two hours away and had visited many times. But I'd never *really* experienced it. The New York I knew was the inside of the Children's Museum, uptown on a Girl Scout trip. Or taking the Martz Trailways bus with my parents to see the Rockefeller Christmas tree. New York meant standing in line in freezing Times Square for half-priced tickets to see *Phantom*. But always with a hand held tight on mine, always guided by the rope they make schoolchildren hold so no one gets misplaced.

During my freshman year of college, I thought I finally had my shot. I scored a paid internship to *Seventeen* magazine. I'd be living in Manhattan for a solid month over Christmas break, working for a magazine I had read fanatically since the age of eleven. Just seeing it peeking out of the mailbox would incite a Pavlovian response in me.

Seventeen was not just a magazine. It was a harbinger of all that might await me out there in young womanhood—dream dates, unflattering swimsuits, Hard Candy nail polish, disordered eating. I tore into it like a starving person.

My mother discovered a great deal on a place to stay. She knew someone with a rent-controlled apartment on the Upper West Side and a teenage daughter leaving for college. I moved right into her room with a pink canopy bed, an *NSYNC poster, and a curfew that wasn't explicit but implied. The window in her bedroom looked out onto an air shaft, and it made me feel like there was just a brick wall waiting outside for me, instead of all the magic of New York.

The internship turned out to be a disappointment, too. Most of my tasks were secretarial—sorting through the sweepstakes mail, organizing the cosmetic closet, licking stamps for the fiction editor's rejection letters. For lunch, the other interns and I would eat at one of those giant midtown cafeterias, which at first impressed me with its dazzling variety of international cuisines, but after the first week it seemed like a giant cosmopolitan pig trough, everything slopped into Styrofoam and weighed by the pound at the end.

At night I'd return to my mom's friend's apartment to sleep under the canopy bed and feel sick about all the magic and romance that I was certain was swirling around out there without me, and before I knew it, the internship was over and it was time to head back to the dorm. I never got a chance to experience the city, to understand the books, the poems, the Lou Reed lyrics.

But now, looking out of the fourth-floor window of the American Apparel company apartment, a different city seemed to be waiting for me. It was four years after 9/11 and the Lower East Side was covered with a fresh coat of paint and full of expensive coffee shops and vegan restaurants. It was a brand-new city, and I was new, too, with a sense of purpose and a real job to do this time.

I envisioned all the girls out there, waiting for me to scout them, turn them on with the promise of progress, and hand over the same card that was given to me only six months ago. *Come join our team.*

I looked out that window into New York City and knew it was truly mine this time.

I just hadn't been ready for it before, but I was now.

III

The next morning, Shuli handed me a folder of résumés she had been collecting in the store. On the top of the stack was a gorgeous Ford model.

Shuli presented her Polaroid with pride.

"Dov loves when we snag a Ford girl," she said.

But one glimpse at her résumé told me the girl had no retail experience. She looked like the perfect AA Classic Girl of course, in her regulation halter bodysuit and a gap-toothed smile. But how long was a Ford model going to stay when she realized that working retail was really just a job, and not a photoshoot?

I flipped through the rest of the stack. Right away, I could see that none of these girls would do. I politely tucked the stack of résumés into my bag but knew I'd never look at them again. I needed hard workers like the LA girls, not just girls who looked the part. Girls who needed the money and the hours and the health insurance. Girls who were hungry for opportunity. Girls like me and Caralee.

I knew just where to find them. And it was within walking distance.
Urban Outfitters.

I knew better than anyone that an Urban employee would be overworked, underpaid, and pushed to the brink of a nearly existential disillusionment. But I also knew that they'd be extremely experienced from the high-volume chaos a store like that churns through daily. They'd be ideal employees, just ripe for the picking.

I headed down Houston Street. It was just four blocks from American Apparel to Urban, which was no accident. Caralee had told me that when Dov was searching for the location for his Lower East Side flagship, he'd hired a rickshaw to take him up and down the streets, searching the FOR RENT signs for the perfect location that could siphon Urban's foot traffic.

I spent the afternoon sitting clandestinely on a bench outside— infiltrating enemy turf. I was a spy in spandex on a secret mission, my stack of scouting cards and my Polaroid camera obscured in my tote. Anytime someone came out showing the telltale signs of retail management—a lanyard around the neck, a key dangling from a wrist—I'd assess her style quick as a flash before she could step off the curb and disappear into the bustle of the city. Then, if she was right, I'd pounce.

Urban employees could go either way. Most of them were overstyled—too hair-cutty, too much eyeliner. The vibes rolling off them were ones of *un*fuckability, for sure. Lots of them were covered in tattoos, which I already knew repelled Dov.

"Tattoos are so dated," I'd hear him say. "So *nineties*."

Facial piercings made him visibly shudder.

But every once in a while a girl would stroll out the Urban doors, looking like a blank canvas. No makeup, a head of long, unstyled hair. Eyebrows unplucked, nails unpolished. No bra. Her rightness would ring out like a bell, and I began to see the clean, brandless Classic Girl there. The American Apparel garments would transpose over her in my mind, as if she were a paper doll. I'd hand her a card, and she'd always take the job.

For the first time in my life, I felt like a powerful woman.

A few days later, word came back that my new hires pleased Dov. I was surprised with how easy it all had been. I found all the girls he needed in one afternoon, and I didn't even have to buy a MetroCard.

I knew this was the start of big things for me.

I was carving out a special kind of job for myself, a much better one than I had back in the shops. I wouldn't be slaving for ten hours a day for Anarah in retail prison, busying myself with the matters of switching out hangers and lightbulbs or clearing out the dressing rooms. I would simply hire the girls who would, and move on to the next city, and do it all over again.

That's how I would make Dov proud. That's how *I* would be rewarded. I wouldn't have to be a Dov girl to climb the ladder. I could get there on my own.

7

The Cruiser

Dov said to go to Boston next and do it all over again.

The order didn't come directly from him but from Ivy back at the Factory, her voice streaming out of my brand-new clamshell Nextel phone, which had chirped to life as soon as I'd opened the box.

I felt a solemn sense of pride when the phone showed up at the New York apartment—I was really an important member of the family now. But the Nextel had a walkie-talkie function that could engage at any moment, so now I was never truly alone. The voices of Caralee, Ivy, Dov—anyone with a company phone—could stream into my consciousness at the push of a button. The first night I got it, I was awoken by the voice of a confused Factory foreman who had the wrong extension.

Still, it was one less bill to worry about each month. Just another way the company was taking care of me. I liked thinking about it that way.

I had only been in New York for a week, but Ivy told me it was time to move on to the next city in need—the new Cambridge shop opening in Harvard Square, Boston's second store. Ivy explained that there weren't any company apartments there yet, so I'd be staying in a hotel.

"You might be there for a while," Ivy said, her voice warping with static. "We'll need an entire staff, since we're starting from scratch."

"From scratch?" I asked. "I have to hire *everyone*?"

"Everyone," she confirmed.

This was clearly a way bigger gig than my New York assignment. I'd be responsible for filling every position on the roster from management on down to backstock, and that meant I was also responsible for a huge part of the fledging store's success.

The pressure was on, but I was ready for it.

"Shouldn't be too hard," Ivy said, practically reading my mind. "It's a college town. Everyone will know the brand."

I asked when my flight would be—I was going to have to get used to traveling at a moment's notice—but Ivy said I'd be picking up a company car and driving there myself.

"Look out your window," she instructed.

I looked down out of the curtainless company apartment window and saw a FASTPARK sign pointing to a parking lot on the other side of Orchard Street. It was filled with an array of 1970s VW Rabbits, 1980s Mercedes, and 1990s Cadillacs—Dov's collection of company cars he'd accumulated over the past three years since the birth of the brand, Ivy explained.

Company cars were like company apartments—another ingenious way to save cash on the traveling girls. No dorky Ford Fiesta rentals here, no expensive contracts, no additional insurance packages—just take whatever you need from Dov's personal fleet and get rolling. I felt a huge smile creep across my face as I realized I wouldn't be freaking out in a Super-Shuttle tomorrow morning—I'd be riding to Boston in style.

I thought about my Honda Civic stick shift back in LA, waiting for me like Cinderella's shitty pumpkin. My life was changing so quickly, it really was starting to seem like a fairy tale. A free phone, a cool car, a bottomless expense account—all of it made me high.

I started to thank Ivy. I wanted her to know how grateful I was, how much I appreciated everything she had done for me so far, but she cut me off.

"We'll always give you everything you need, as long as you're working here," she said. "We'll always hook it up."

The Nextel gave one final chirp and went silent. I was alone in the room now.

III

The parking attendant was waiting for me.

He scanned a pegboard and swiped a pair of keys from it with a practiced hand.

"Ah, yes," he said, giving me a strange smile before disappearing into the lot.

Was it the smile of a creeper? I couldn't tell, even though I was hardwired to identify them by now. It was a hot day in the last gasp of summer, and by noon the heat seemed to rise from the sidewalk itself. I wasn't wearing much, since I was anticipating a long, hot, boring car ride in traffic. I rolled my eyes. *Typical.*

But when the car arrived, I knew exactly what was cooking behind the attendant's creepy smile.

It wasn't a Mercedes that rolled out. And it definitely wasn't a crummy Volkswagen.

It was a 1993 Ford Crown Victoria police cruiser.

Just seeing it raised all the hair on my arms.

It was an unmarked cop car that Dov had bought secondhand at the Canadian car auctions in his hometown of Montreal, and it was heading right for me, sleek and imposing as a shark. It didn't say POLICE anywhere on it, but its authority was unmistakable—if you saw it idling on the side of the highway, you'd slow down.

Ivy was right, again—this car was the ultimate hookup. As I settled into the cushy driver's seat, I saw there was a switch on the dash that made red and blue lights flash through its grille, and another that unleashed the earsplitting wail of a siren.

Holy shit.

I had a sneaking suspicion that Dov had meant for *me* to have this specific car, to feel its absolute power underneath me as I zoomed up the coast, growing our kingdom girl by girl.

I typed the destination of the Boston store—330 Newbury Street—into the car's TomTom. I figured I'd get started there. I licked my finger to adhere its suction cup to the windshield.

ROUTE CALCULATING, it said.

I sat back in my seat, and my eyes wandered to the side-view mirror.

A girl burst out of the doorway of the American Apparel store. She craned her neck in the direction of the parking lot, and took off running in my direction, waving her hands over her head.

Had I forgotten something? My cards, my Polaroid camera, my new phone—everything I needed was right here beside me on the passenger seat.

I rolled down the window.

"WAIT!" the girl screeched. She was tall, her long legs loping over the crosswalk, and she reached me in seconds. "HOLD UP!"

She had an overstuffed duffel swaying from her shoulder and tiny baby bangs framing a teenage face.

"Oh my god, I almost missed you," she said, opening the back door of the cruiser and throwing in her bag. "And you are like, *my escape.*"

I looked at her, bewildered.

Who was *this*?

No one had mentioned anything about anyone coming with me. This Boston trip was going to be *my* chance to prove to everyone—but mainly Dov—how capable I was in my new role as a scout, hiring an entire store on my own. I didn't need any help, I didn't want anyone else taking the credit. I wanted to show how far *I* could go if given the opportunity. How valuable I was to the company.

Now I had another teenager on my watch, just like back at the Sunset store.

I gritted my teeth and tried to mask my annoyance with a smile.

"I'm Jade," she said, collapsing into the passenger seat. "Dov said I could come."

III

Jade and I were stuck in a nasty clog of traffic on the George Washington Bridge, inching our way out of the city, when she suggested we give the siren a try.

She had already been testing my patience—putting her giant feet on the dashboard, dropping my phone in the bottomless crevasse between the seat and the console, and then scattering popcorn everywhere during the recovery effort.

And now she wanted to test the siren?

"Lemme just *doooo it*," she whined. "It probably doesn't even work. All the company cars have something wrong with them."

I'd find out in the coming months that this was all very true. A broken radio, windows that wouldn't roll down, fraying seat belts—company cars were always janked. Dov hunted for a deal and knew the girls wouldn't complain. We weren't the complaining type.

"*Pleeeeeeease*. Lemme just try!"

The old me wanted to warn Jade about how dangerous it would be to use the siren. Impersonating a police officer? I was sure that was a big deal. We'd get arrested or fined or imprisoned. It was probably a federal thing. I certainly didn't want to have to call *my parents* from a New York City jail. Didn't she know how humiliating that would be?

But then it hit me.

I wouldn't have to call my parents. I would just call Dov. With his deep pockets and deeper disdain for all and any authority aside from his own, I knew he'd come to our rescue. And here I was, stuck with this annoying teenager for who knows how long—on a car ride through hell, which my TomTom was actually identifying as northern New Jersey.

"Fucking press it." I sighed.

She flipped the switch, and a deafening alarm wailed out from the depths of the car.

WEEEEEE-OOOOOOOOOOO WEEEEEEEEE-OOOOOOOOO URNHH URNN URHNN!

Oh my god. It was LOUD.

Immediately the traffic cleaved in front of us like a streak of water in oil. Cars began to wedge into the next lane over, absorbing into the gridlock. Where once there had been a total impasse, now there was a way forward.

My body buzzed with the feeling of doing something forbidden, and getting away with it.

Jade and I eased our way into New England, using the switch sparingly and only when we really needed it. But even better than whizzing past the wall of traffic was catching a glimpse of the astonished faces of the other drivers as they obediently heeded our siren song and got the hell out of our way. We were two girls, screaming with laughter, stripped down to bikini tops in an unmarked police car with all the windows down. The only flaw with the cruiser was that its air-conditioning was broken, of course.

Maybe Jade wasn't so bad, I realized. I never would have had the guts to hit the switch myself, never would have had this much fun on my own. Our ride in the cruiser was really bonding us together—we were nearing Boston when she blurted out the real reason why she was tagging along on my scouting trip.

Last spring, she had done a nude shoot with a famous photographer and filmmaker who palled around with Dov, and the photos had made their way to a popular art mag that was circulating through the city that summer.

"Which photographer?" I asked.

I'd heard rumors about Terry Richardson hanging out at the Factory with Dov. They seemed like two peas in pod—the same muttonchops, the same nerdy glasses, the same familial nicknames. *Uncle Terry, Daddy Dov.*

"It was Larry Clark," she said.

I groaned.

I knew all about Larry Clark. Gia and Elyse from the Sunset shop had shot Clark's 2005 Supreme calendar—twelve barely legal, fully nude girls holding skateboards instead of riding them. The shots didn't sit well with me—they looked like kiddie porn. Some of the girls were flat-chested and *so* young-looking. Creepy.

Gia told me she'd accepted a low rate to do the shoot because her understanding was the calendar was licensed for a limited release in Japan. Whether that was the case, Clark and Supreme sold them in the United States and Europe and wherever else they pleased, using all the shots just as indiscriminately. Elyse's nude shot was repurposed for a Supreme T-shirt and printed on the undersides of skate decks, which she said hadn't been part of the deal, either.

Gia went to one of Clark's art openings and saw that he was selling all the shots he took of her that day—not just the one from the calendar— for a hundred bucks a pop.

"I bought one," Gia said. "I didn't know what else to do."

That was another reason the shots were so skeevy—the photos looked exploitative because the girls were being *exploited*.

"Yeah, well, I didn't like my shots, either," Jade said, gazing out of the cruiser's window. "They're embarrassing. And all the girls at the shop are making fun of me for shooting them."

Jade covered her face.

"I think I look ugly in them," she said. "I wish I never did them, but now it's too late."

I couldn't believe it.

Not her regret over the sleazy shots—that I understood. The party shots from my bathtub still lingered like a dark shadow—I couldn't be sure where they'd turn up next. But what shocked me was that the NYC American Apparel girls were teasing her about them. It bowled me over—it seemed so at odds with the brand's message. The only sex-shaming behavior I had witnessed since my start with the company was the time I taped up a topless ad of Caralee in the Sunset shop bathroom, and the cleaning lady hung a towel over it.

"I needed a break from the girls, so Dov said I could scout Boston with you," Jade said.

In that moment, any lingering annoyance I felt about Jade disappeared. I was here to make her feel better, to guide her—I was going to have to be her big sister now.

"Screw those girls, Jade. They haven't evolved yet," I told her. "That's just *puritanical tribalism*."

That was a phrase I started hearing around the shop after the *Jane* mag flyerbombing. I wasn't exactly sure what it meant, but it sounded applicable in this situation.

I told Jade they were just a bunch of mean girls bringing her down to make themselves feel better.

"Oldest story in the book," I said. Jade was still looking out the window, deep in thought.

I puzzled over how different the American Apparel girls could be here in New York—it seemed the farther we got from the source, the more the company ethos was getting diluted. What was happening to the sex positivity we were celebrating in the Golden State? It was transforming into something toxic over here on the Beast Coast.

The stores looked exactly the same on the inside. The iPod pumped the same jams—early Prince, late Talking Heads. We had the same propaganda hung on the walls, printed on the back of the city weeklies. But here in New York, it was all starting to seem like an elaborate set. This wasn't the American Apparel I knew. It just looked like it.

I was grateful for the Los Angeles stores, where everything was real.

I tugged a joint from my wallet and offered it to Jade, and in just a few minutes, we were both feeling upbeat again.

III

We were just outside Boston, or maybe somewhere underneath it, when I saw the flash of lights in my rearview and the sobering *whoop-whoop* of a real cruiser's siren right behind us.

Immediately my hands began to sweat on the steering wheel. Oh no, had I been speeding back there in Connecticut? The car's odometer ran in kilometers, so I couldn't ever be sure how fast I was going.

We were in that disorienting maze of subterranean highway tunnels that crept under the bay and into the city, and I started thinking about all the terrible things we had been doing on our trip. *Oh God!* Why had I been so stupid? Of course using the siren was illegal.

I pulled to the side of the road and watched the traffic cruelly passing us by, craning their necks, curious as to why one police car would be pulling over another.

"Jade," I whispered.

She reached forward and opened the glove box. A cascade of parking tickets flowed out, left behind by former irresponsible drivers who were also sure that Dov would take care of everything.

"Oh, shit," she said, scrambling to shove them back in.

I avoided the temptation to instantly blame her. I wanted to scream—"This was all *your* idea!" But looking over at her, ashen and terrified in the passenger seat, I realized I had to be the brave one. I was the adult here. The one with the driver's license. I took a deep breath and sat up in the driver's seat, ready to face my punishment.

The cop's flashlight was winking through the dimness of the murky tunnel as he approached us. The headlights on his car were stretching him out like a shadow puppet, and by the time he got to my window, he had swallowed up all the light in the tunnel.

What was going to happen to me now?

He leaned into my window, smirking. He was so close I could smell his aftershave.

"You girls lost or somethin'?"

Lost? *Yes, lost!* That was a good angle to take here.

"We're *so* lost. Right, Jade?" I looked over at her. She nodded like a dashboard doll, *yes yes yes, we're lost lost lost.*

"Woo-weee," he said, sweeping his flashlight over the backseat.

Jade and I waited, petrified with fear. Where was that roach that we'd split an hour ago, so confident we were untouchable?

The cop ran a finger along the driver-side door's contour and smiled. He certainly was enjoying this.

I breathed in deeply—it *did* smell like weed in here.

I met Jade's gaze but couldn't hold it there. I felt like I might start crying at any moment.

The cop let out a low whistle.

"You never see 'em like this anymore. What a *beaut.* Nowadays it's all Chargers, but there's nothing like a Crown Vic."

My eyes met with Jade's again. She was smiling. I let a welcome wave of relief knock me over. The police officer hadn't pulled us over because we had broken the rules.

He wanted to talk about the stupid car!

"I shouldn't be telling you girls this, but these beasts can turn on a dime at a hundred miles per hour. That's why I love 'em. Just a quality piece of high-performance machinery, right?"

I nodded, playing it cool. I felt all the tension drain out of my shoulders. We were going to be OK.

The cop began waxing about his early days on the force in his Crown Vic—he really was only interested in talking about himself. And we were happy to be his captive audience—just two cute, lost shopgirls. Nothing to see, or smell, here. Some chivalry switch turned on in him right away.

"I'll do you gals a solid," he said. "Just follow me and I'll getcha where you need to go."

He escorted us the last few miles to the Newbury Street shop, sirens and lights flashing. We cut through the rush-hour traffic like a hot knife.

Who could stop us now?

No one.

III

Jade and I made light work of Boston. It didn't take long to scout a new staff for the Harvard store. We picked the most experienced workers from a stack of résumés waiting for us at the Newbury shop, pilfered a few managers from Urban, scouted a few MassArt girls on the T, and turned in their Polaroids to the Factory in a week's time.

I was good at scouting on my own, but together, Jade and I evoked a sort of hipster gravitational pull, drawing all the right kind of people into our orbit. The New England girls were just our type—with their unstyled hair that fell to their waists and their modest maxi skirts, they reminded me of Salem witches. A different, spookier flavor of the Classic Girl. We scooped them easily from Urban, from Newbury Comics, from the ritzy boutiques that lined Boston's Back Bay.

Jade and I picked up groceries at Bread & Circus—things that would stay good overnight in our shared hotel room. A loaf of sprouted bread, a jar of natural peanut butter, stiff as concrete. A basket of strawberries so lovely and fragrant they made our hotel room smell like bubble gum.

We saved all our receipts, of course, but Jade had developed a way of gaming the system that she was eager to share with me. The trick was to dig through the trash to find the discarded receipt of someone who had enjoyed a far more opulent lunch than you that day.

"I don't know about you, but I can only afford a green bar and a juice with my weekly paycheck, but look—"

Jade pulled a greasy receipt out of the trash can and waved it triumphantly over her head. "Some lucky bastard had a quinoa bowl and shrimp spring rolls *and* a kombucha. That's the kind of lunch that will pay off in the long run."

Jade told me some of the wilier girls in New York even used the store cash registers as their own personal ATMs, going through the motions of returning something and then pocketing the cash.

"But isn't that stealing?" I asked. "Aren't they afraid they'll get caught?"

Jade laughed.

"By who? No one's really keeping track of stuff like that," she said.

There were all kinds of ways to get ahead on the road, some dirtier than others. I'd have to learn to do it my own way, because I knew I was never heading back to work in the stores again. Ivy called with our next assignment—drive the cruiser to Connecticut and do it all over *again* for the new Yale store opening in New Haven.

"It might be tricky to hire in the summer," Ivy said.

"No problem," I told her. "We got this."

I already had a method in mind I'd tried out in Boston—exclusively hiring townies who'd stick with the job long after school was out for the summer. This was the only "vision" in my scouting practices, really. Just common sense. But it seemed to be working for me—Ivy told me next was Philly, then Richmond, then Charlotte. I envisioned our route snaking down the coast, me and Jade speeding along it in the cruiser.

Jade was just as excited as I was for our trip. We fantasized about all the deserving assholes we'd scare the shit out of with the cruiser. We'd swing by every frat house in North America, hit that siren, and watch them scatter like cockroaches!

With the cruiser, the possibilities were endless. I couldn't wait for us to get started.

Later that night, as we were packing up the room to leave and I was making peanut butter sandwiches for the road, Jade's Nextel chirped and she disappeared into the bathroom.

There was a marathon of *The Girls Next Door* blaring from the TV that I was only half watching, but in a moment of silence—Holly Madison contemplatively chewing on a strand of blond hair—I heard a sound that I knew very well.

"*Nooooooo,*" Jade whined.

When she opened the door and came out, she looked deflated.

"I need a ride to South Station," she said. "Right now."

The last bus to New York left in an hour, and she needed to be on it.

"What? *Nooooo.*" Now I was the one whining.

"But we're leaving tomorrow," I said. "We still have so much left to do!"

All those girls, in all those cities, waiting for us to scout them. All those receipts, waiting to be dug out of the trash. We'd be in the cruiser driving full throttle—a hundred miles an hour and turning on a dime—leaving behind those terrible girls who bullied her.

Now she wanted to go back . . . to them?

"How could you leave now, when we're just getting started?"

"I just need to go," she said, folding her arms. We sat in awkward silence the entire drive to the bus station and didn't hit the siren even once.

When I came back to the hotel, the room felt emptier than ever. Only the lingering odor of strawberries remained, a few overripe stragglers moldering in the trash.

Jade had forgotten her silver ring on the nightstand. I slipped it on my finger. It was an unusual ring made of silver mesh, with a clasp like a belt and three little notches where the prong slides through. There was a ghostly indenture where Jade had worn it on the tightest setting, so it would fit her little finger.

I felt very alone.

For the past week, Jade and I were the ones in charge, high on the kind of power I had never experienced before, sirens blazing. But now the trip stretching out in front of me had turned imposing, overwhelming. Could I really do this all on my own?

Right before she disappeared through the glass doors of South Station, I wanted to beg her to stay, and I almost did, until I realized it would be of no use. I didn't know who she was talking to in the bathroom, but I had my suspicions.

Daddy—the real authority—had spoken, so Jade had to go.

I never saw her again.

8

≡

The Boys

The Yale store wasn't just a scouting assignment—it turned out there was a little more to it than that. The morning I arrived in the cruiser, I received a chirp from the Factory instructing me to meet with a local real estate agent in New Haven to tour a potential location for the new store. If it looked like a good spot, I'd give the OK, and the Factory would take it from there.

I was confident about my scouting and hiring ability after my successes in New York and Boston, but I had *no clue* what went into picking a new store location. I figured I'd better just keep my mouth shut and take a stab at it. Really, how hard could it be? All the stores were basically the same—a couple of coats of white paint and neon signage could transform any old brick-and-mortar into a recognizable part of our realm.

But when I showed up to the address, the "store" waiting for me was still in the very early stages of construction. It was just a glorified cement hole in the ground, surrounded by a framework of joists that made me feel like I was walking around a 3D cube and not an American Apparel store at all. I started feeling hot prickles of panic—who thought I had the qualifications to make a top-dollar decision like this? Was it Ivy, telling everyone at the Factory how competent I was? Or Dov, thinking my hiring vision could extend into all facets of business? What if I made a mistake and blew everything with this one decision, which I had no qualifications to make?

I figured I better start thinking like a businessman—how would Dov approach this?

Location, location, location, he'd say.

The store's locale was what was important here—any old dump could get a makeover. I stuck to the facts—the site was in downtown New Haven on Broadway, a few short blocks from Yale's campus. It was also directly next to an Apple store. I thought about all those progressive Ivy League coeds streaming past this alluring new storefront on their way to the Genius Bar. *Cha-ching.*

The real estate agent stared at me as I introduced myself.

"Will anyone else be joining us today?" he asked, raising his eyebrows.

He was wearing a three-piece suit. I was wearing a micro mini and flip-flops.

"Nope," I said, deadpanning. "Just me."

It seemed like this obsolete Gen-Xer was going to need a dose of feminist reckoning, Millennial-style. Why couldn't a representative from a hugely successful corporation be a young woman in a miniskirt? I was here to make a million-dollar decision, so he had better wipe that surprise off his face.

"Please excuse me," he said politely, handing me a hard hat. "May I show you around?"

He had no choice but to take me seriously, and it felt *so good.*

I signed off on the Yale location, got back in the cruiser, and rolled on to Philly, where I doled out jobs to all my old comrades for the new store opening on Walnut Street in Rittenhouse Square. The location was only a block from the Urban Outfitters offices where I languished not even a year before. I wanted to yell at the windows, *Look at me now, Beverly! See how I'm thriving?* Urban had overlooked the value of my youth and potential, stuffing me away in a cubicle and never giving me a shot to truly spread my wings. Thank God I had gotten out of there when I had the chance.

After Philly was Richmond—another full staff locked down for the new store in the Carytown district. Then it was back to New York to drop the cruiser off and fly back home to LA to await my next assignment.

I'd been on the road for a month. The first thing I did when I got back was turn in my receipts. Three days later, $875 was deposited into my checking account, on top of my regular earnings. *Ahh.* What a relief. Expensing my life while traveling was making me significantly more money than just working in the stores. I paid rent to my roommate in cash and didn't bother unpacking my bag. A week later, I was on my way to Tempe, Arizona, to do it all over again.

Everything about traveling for American Apparel felt incredible.

Giving out high-paying jobs, picking locations where the brand would take root, getting the occasional pat on the back from the Factory about my dedication—it only made me ambitious for more. I never missed a single Nextel chirp, even if it was in the middle of the night. Once I left my phone in my hotel room when I showered, and came out to twenty-three missed calls from Dov—he had kept the phone continuously ringing until I answered—telling me I was needed in Palo Alto immediately to scout for the Stanford store, since Yale had gone so well. I never made that mistake again—the phone went wherever I did, and I dropped everything for a call from it, a dog loyal to its master.

The scouting job also came with unexpected perks—the little bit of celebrity I carried with me as the first American Apparel girl to land in each city was rewarded with invitations to house parties, rides to cool bars, and offerings of the best locally sourced weed. I rolled so many joints on the onion-skin pages of hotel Gideons Bibles, I could papier-mâché my own staircase to hell. But at the end of each night, I'd still end up alone in my room at the Days Inn—only big cities had company apartments—and a familiar loneliness would creep back in.

Sometimes I'd get a chirp from Caralee in the middle of the night, and that always made me feel less like a satellite drifting through space. We'd walkie-talkie back and forth about our adventures, the new cities where we were planting the seeds of our realm.

By that fall of 2005, there were seventy-five American Apparel stores dotting the globe—thirty of them internationally—and their locations were getting more glamorous as they became more remote. But it was beginning to dawn on me that I was getting assigned the second-string cities that no one else wanted. When Caralee was on a scouting mission in Tel Aviv, I was on one in Milwaukee. When Ivy flew off to kick-start Tokyo, I was jet-setting to Baltimore. Dov girls always got first pick, but I was still happy for their scraps. I told myself I'd get to the exciting cities eventually—I just had to pay my dues first.

Caralee never seemed lonely on the road. Her job was more of a training manager than a scout—she'd stick around in the new stores for the first month to make sure they went off without a hitch, training the girls and partying with them, too. I'd pore over the shots on Myspace the next morning, green with envy. My job was always performed solitarily—scouting, interviewing, and hiring, and then flying out to the next city, where I'd start everything over again. I had no time to build friendships on the road like she did.

One night she chirped me while I was in Charlotte, and right away she could tell I was feeling down.

"I'm lonely," I told her.

"Lonely on the road?" Caralee said, dumbfounded.

It was a concept that had never occurred to her.

"Call up some boys, have a great night." She told me that Dov encouraged the girls to date other employees.

"It's better to keep it in the family," she said.

III

The first one was William.

I discovered him in Charlotte when I held an open call for a full staff. He was a hunky, substantial, blue-collar kind of guy. He had big hands and a thundering southern drawl that made me want to wrap my legs around him—I could just imagine one of his ancestors pushing a plow.

It was my last night in Charlotte, and William's last night working as a pizza delivery boy. Tomorrow morning he'd start his new job training as the backstock manager for the new American Apparel in SouthPark, and I'd be flying to Gainesville, Florida.

I took a page from Caralee's book and thought, *Why the hell not?* If Dov had no qualms about dating his subordinates, why should I? I called up William and invited him over for a drink.

When he showed up half an hour later with a six-pack of Bud Light and a rose ripped from a bush on his walk over, I began to see how the rest of the evening could take shape for me.

After I flew out tomorrow morning, I'd never come back to Charlotte.

And here was William—already hired, so I didn't have to feel like a creep on the casting couch—with a rose and a bashful smile and six feet of tall, sturdy manliness I wanted to scale like a tree. After two cans of lukewarm beer, I leaned in and kissed him. It was the first time I'd ever made the first move on someone new.

Soon all of our clothes were off, and William's body was emanating heat under my naked skin like metal in the sun. Slipping into sex with him felt natural, so completely different from all the sex I'd had before with my cheater ex, which always felt phony and orchestrated—the machinations of a porn he'd seen in which I'd been cast as an extra, fumbling through a scene that wasn't written for me.

But sleeping with William was totally different. We had no history, and since it was our last night together, we had no future either. I didn't need to be self-conscious about anything. I felt empowered to ask for everything I wanted—and William enthusiastically gave it to me. We were *talking* to each other, joking around as we got each other off. We were both laughing, tipsy on fuckjoy. I was surprised how comfortable I could feel with a stranger.

At one point, he laughed, and a bit of self-consciousness flared up in me.

"What's wrong?" I asked.

"Nothing," he said, sighing and scratching a patch of golden hair on his chest. "It's just kinda crazy that I'm having sex with someone I have *no business* having sex with."

My heart stopped.

Had I gone too far? Was he having doubts about sleeping with someone who hired him? Did he think I was abusing my power? I was ready to tell him what Caralee had told me—*It's better to keep it in the family*.

"Just someone like you, I mean," William said. "Like, an American Apparel girl."

It was the highest form of compliment—I gave him a long, sexy kiss.

For the past six months I'd been with the company, I always felt this big divide stretching out between the girl I thought I was and the woman I wanted to be. But William hadn't been able to tell the difference—the two were beginning to merge into the same person. When we were finally through, I slept soundly, like I had exorcised a terrible demon and could start the rest of my life now.

I got up early the next morning to catch my SuperShuttle and left

William sleeping there in my hotel room. Before I left, I pulled out my Polaroid and took a snap. He looked like a little angel sleeping in the white sheets. Tousled blond hair, his hand resting over his heart, his mouth hanging open.

I located the pad of hotel stationery by the phone—DAYS INN, CHARLOTTE, NORTH CAROLINA—and uncapped the pen with my teeth.

Dear William, I wrote.

Had such fun. Good luck with the shop.

I chewed on the cap.

Sleep in and order whatever you want.

It was something I'd seen in a movie, *Pretty Woman* maybe? The cinematic trope where if a powerful businessman leaves his sleeping paramour in his hotel bed, it was customary to offer breakfast. Except I was the Richard Gere now—the much better end of the deal.

From then on, I would try out anyone I desired. I had nothing to feel naive about anymore, I'd left that girl behind when I started working for American Apparel. If any of my scouts showed a modicum of interest, I set them in my crosshairs, and by my last night in town, I was seeing the most romantic parts of every city in the most romantic time to see them—the last twelve hours before I'd fly out. I smooched in the moonlight by the full-scale Parthenon model in Nashville, on the *Lost Boys* bridge in Santa Cruz. I rolled on the Astroturf of the University of Florida stadium in the middle of the night, scoring on the field despite never having been one for sports.

I started calling this period of my life *The Year I Fucked Everybody*.

Factually it stretched out far longer than a year, but it's easier to refer to it roundly that way. Like how John Lennon's Lost Weekend in LA was really eighteen months.

The Year I Fucked Everybody was an era.

III

How many people did I scout? How many did I hire and bring into the company during those early years? Some rough mental arithmetic leads me to a number over five hundred, but less than a thousand. All the girls I scouted on the road tend to blend together into one Alpha American Apparel girl, since there were so many of them—but it's the boys I remember the best. Maybe because hiring them was so much more difficult.

If Dov had his way, I would hire none at all.

"Don't hire any fuckin' guys," he'd tell me, through gritted teeth. He regarded all of them suspiciously, turf invaders, coming to pillage the kingdom he created.

But, of course, I had to hire guys. It was a necessary evil, especially in those early days when I was scouting a store from scratch. We needed them to lift the boxes, to do light security detail, and walk the girls out at night. We needed them to pick up our lunches on their skateboards, to light our cigarettes with their Zippos. We needed guys.

I learned from experience that the only way to hire guys successfully was to seek out Dov look-alikes—Mini Dovs—clean-cut dorks in button-down oxfords. Abercrombie dudes, Gap dudes, the blander the better. They always got the thumbs-up, as if he was living vicariously through them in each new city. He detested the dyed black hair and architectured hairstyles of the emo look du jour. If he detected a hint of eyeliner on a guy in a Polaroid—no matter how bleached out the flash had made it—it was curtains for them and the hapless scout who dared to try and sneak one by.

"No *pierced protestors*!" he'd rage.

I never made mistakes like that—I was the girl with the vision. After I had a few stores under my belt, I didn't even have to submit Polaroids anymore. I'd still take one and turn it in with their completed application and résumé, but I was trusted to bring aboard whoever I wanted. I was good at my job, no one ever questioned my hires.

But no place tested my scouting skills like Tempe, Arizona—not the most hipster-friendly of college towns. For three solid weeks, I camped out there, searching for our kind. Tempe was a homogenous cowboy town with a local bar called the Rustler's Rooste that had a depressed bull in a pen outside, flicking flies. Diverse hires were extremely hard to find, and I was getting desperate.

As a last resort, I posted a flyer in the empty storefront of the new store—the First National Bank of Tempe building, its old bank vault repurposed as dressing rooms. Posting a flyer—with my phone number on it—was a tactic I only used in worst-case scenarios because it broadened the scope of applicants too widely, and my phone would ring constantly.

But in Tempe, posting that flyer paid off.

A drove of nerdy, straitlaced young men showed up to my open call. Dov dream boys. A quick scan through their résumés showed these boys were dependable creatures of retail, but they also appeared to be upstanding pillars of their community. They were Big Brothers, they delivered Meals on Wheels. There was something aggressively wholesome about their extracurriculars, and then I saw something about a *sacred service*, some kind of missionary work. It dawned on me that these weren't just polite college boys on the cutting edge of the impending normcore trend.

They were Mormons.

Real live Mormons who stumbled upon my NOW HIRING sign in the empty storefront and decided to apply to this interesting new company that they were completely unfamiliar with.

"But do you *know* American Apparel?" I asked one. He had a tidy blond crew cut and was wearing the same polo shirt and loafer combo that Dov would breeze through the Factory in.

"Oh, of course!" the Mormon fibbed. "I guarantee I'm the right man for the job."

We both smiled at each other, thinking we knew something the other didn't.

I needed those Mormons. They were almost perfect, aside from being white as Wonder Bread. Still, I needed them. Beggars couldn't be choosers, and I had to find a full staff immediately so I could blow this cowboy town and keep moving. And the Mormons would be the perfect offering for Dov, who had an aversion to organized religion. Subverting religious folk would delight him. I'd be a total legend at the Factory, the top of the pile. Higher than a Dov girl, if there was such a thing.

I had to have them.

Not to have sex with, like the other boys I was getting so comfortable acquiring, but in a way, the Mormons were commodities just the same. I was confident I could snag them, too. I pitched them The Hustle like never before—store management, full benefits, and the humanitarian thrill of working for a progressive company.

This really was doing the Lord's work the 2000s way, wasn't it? They'd run their own little ethical paradise out here in the desert. It was practically biblical.

I could tell I had them on the hook. But as the flash of my Polaroid lit up each of their glowing little cherubic faces, I felt a little pang of dishonesty. I figured I should level with them. I told them they had the best retail job of their lives waiting for them, but they better go home and give the company a Google first.

"If you're still into it, meet me here tomorrow," I said. "And we'll start your paperwork."

That night, alone in my hotel room, I started thinking about what I'd say to Dov about my miraculous acquisition.

"Mormonism is just another brand that's Made in the USA, like American Apparel," I'd tell him. "We even both have the special underwear."

He'd love that.

The next morning I arrived at the store bright and early, but the Mormons never showed. I'm sure they took one look at the website—a shot of a girl hovering over Dov's crotch in blue nylon shorts was the first thing that loaded on the home page—and it told them everything they needed to know about the ethical paradise I had tried to hustle them on.

I stayed in town an extra week, raiding a Hollister and scrounging up a few tatted options at Urban—not my finest work, but Dov would never visit Tempe, anyway. It was too far off the beaten track, a city valuable to him only because of the large state university there that would bring in enough financial flow to cover the rent. The storefront's existence there was basically cheap advertising for the brand.

Opening a store in a city like Tempe was like Buzz Aldrin planting the American flag on the rough terrain of the uninhabitable moonscape—its only purpose was to say, look, American Apparel was here. We've conquered this city, too.

III

In my downtime between trips—which wasn't much, we were opening a store a week by the end of 2005—I had plenty of work to keep me busy hiring for LA. In the same way American Apparel stores were popping up across the country, they were also spreading across the city as quickly. When I left a few weeks earlier, there was only one store on Hollywood Boulevard, but when I returned there were now three, and they all needed my hiring vision.

I'd sift through the hundreds of weekly online applicants who would upload a pic and a résumé, and then I'd call up my selects and invite them to an interview. I'd hold open calls at the two stores on Hollywood Boulevard, which were each exciting in their own right. The shop farthest west was directly across from Grauman's Chinese Theatre—some of the most expensive real estate in the country—and American Apparel had two floors' worth. I loved holding calls there, where the girls could watch all the stars arriving to the movie premieres from their spot at the cash wrap. Everything about the store felt so Hollywood, so touched by celebrity—the store manager was even dating a Wayans brother. I'd see her ducking through paparazzi shots in *Us Weekly* in the American Apparel scoop back minidress.

Farther east was the store at Hollywood and Cherokee, which existed on the more hard-up, weathered portion of the famous boulevard. The musk of decay and nag champa leaked from the dingy storefronts as scuzzy men in superhero costumes patrolled the Walk of Fame, searching for tourists. Crust punks and Vietnam vets jangled Styrofoam cups of change on the corner. It was the land of the three-dollar hot dog.

I loved holding interviews at the Cherokee store because of its grit, not despite it—it was always so fascinating to me that Hollywood is this fabled town of glamour that slides along on a grimy underbelly. There was a bar directly next to the shop, and Danny Bonaduce could always be found perched outside on a stool like an oracle, nursing a pint glass and dying to be recognized by the double-decker tour buses that ran down the boulevard like clockwork.

Danny was fresh off the premiere episode of *Breaking Bonaduce*, his second round of exploitative fame in showbiz, and he was going to make the most of it—fame and infamy in Hollywood are basically the same thing. Sometimes he would offer sage advice, but only for those who could really value it—most of the girls had no idea who Danny was. But I always stopped to pay my respects.

"Danny," I asked one afternoon, "how long will I stay in LA?"

"You, kid?" Danny said, giving me a smile full of yellow teeth. "You're a lifer, just like me."

"You really think so?"

"Of course. In fact, I can feel something special brewing for you today. Something is in the air."

I stopped to sniff the Hollywood Boulevard air. It stunk. Could there really be something magic in the atmosphere for me today? I thanked him and stepped into the shop, where twenty potential new hires waited for me with hopeful faces, clutching résumés.

I lived for the feeling of striding into an open call in my short shorts and slouchy boots, my Polaroid strapped across my chest like a weapon. Line 'em up! I'll take anyone I want. I'd commandeer a dressing room for my office, and call them in for interviews one by one.

That afternoon at Cherokee, a good one caught my eye immediately— a tall, thin *Wassup Rockers* type in a leather jacket, inky black hair in tight ringlets falling down his back like a romance novel cover.

"Let's start with you," I said, pointing at him.

"At your service." He bowed a little.

Together we stepped into the dressing room.

III

Viktor was a Valley boy, born and raised. Muscular as an iguana in the skinniest of jeans. Always with some sort of swollen foot or ankle, a malady from a skateboarding mishap. He was handsome, cool, and flirtatious—my type. When I hired him that day at Cherokee, I knew he'd be the perfect backstock boy, a gift of catnip to the lucky girls working at whichever store I'd place him—Sunset maybe. He was definitely an Echo Park kind of guy. But I figured first, I ought to give him a whirl.

To thank me for his new job, Viktor took me out dancing to Star Shoes in Hollywood. At first, things were looking promising. It was a Northern Soul night, and we danced for hours, clinging to each other in the sweaty din of the club, which was full of shooting bits of light like the inside of a kaleidoscope. Viktor could actually dance, and he'd pick me up and twirl me around like I was full of helium. He was strong and didn't seem to ever tire out—which boded well for the rest of the evening, I thought. Soon we were out of there and in his car, heading back east toward my place.

"Did you have a good time tonight, mama?"

California boys were always calling girls mama. It took some getting used to at first, but I was starting to like it.

I really did have a good time with Viktor that night. And as he was paying the tab, I caught a glimpse of gold sticking out of his wallet—a Magnum condom, unmistakable. I wondered if Viktor was one of the guys who really needed a Magnum, or one of the guys who just think that they do.

I had to find out. I reached over and patted his thigh gently.

"I sure did, Vik," I said. It really had been a great night, and it was only just beginning.

"I'm glad, because that's one of my favorite places to JESUS FUCK-ING CHRIST WHAT THE HELL IS WRONG WITH YOU???"

Viktor slammed on his brakes as my seat belt tightened around me like a boa constrictor. A clunky sedan had cut us off. I could see the blazing taillights and the bald head of a senior citizen at the wheel.

"That MOTHERFUCKER," Viktor said, screeching over a lane. "Let's see how *he* likes it."

I grabbed for the door handle to steady myself as the car accelerated and looked over at Viktor. He was hunkered down over the steering wheel, eyebrows knitted in a death glare. He looked like a guy driving a tank in an action movie, not a guy on his way to get laid.

A road rager. Ugh, such a turnoff.

My body swayed in my seat as he careened in front of the other car and slammed on his breaks. What the hell was wrong with him?

"It's just an old man! Relax!" I cried.

What had happened to the suave skater boy who was slow-dancing with me to Sam Cooke a half hour ago? He had transformed into an immature brat, all his sexy coolness disappearing immediately—he became completely *unfuckable*. But when we arrived at my place and he walked me to the door, I still invited him in. We'd spent all night together, and now he was here, so I figured I'd better at least give him a spin to see what that Magnum was about, and that would be the end of it. I didn't really want to, but I would.

It was *The Year I Fucked Everybody*, I wasn't thinking clearly.

Once we were inside, I made the best of things and headed straight for his zipper.

Most of the dicks I'd known had been moderate specimens, but Viktor's sprung from his zipper like a prank snake-in-a-can. All his bad behavior from earlier was momentarily forgotten. He carried me into my bedroom knock-kneed, his skinny jeans stuck halfway down his legs, and threw me down on the bed like a pro wrestler. But that was where the fun ended for me.

Viktor was strictly business. There were no opening ceremonies, no communication about what I was into. Just the flash of the Magnum wrapper, and then Viktor behind the wheel again—ramming me over and over with all the finesse of a teenager learning to drive a stick shift.

We had just started, but I was ready to be done. Viktor was the kind of guy who rested on the laurels of simply having a big dick, but he possessed no technique. He was here to get off, and that was it. I tried to maintain some semblance of control by getting on top, but the feeling of desperately trying to stay upright while he fucked me from below kept reminding me of that one humiliating time I had tried to ride the mechanical bull at the Saddle Ranch.

I needed to get off this ride immediately. I faked a big operatic orgasm, hoping that would be the end of it, and rolled off, panting. I could feel the beginnings of a headache cooking, my brain battered from all the jackhammering.

Viktor smiled over at me, pleased with himself.

"Don't worry, mama," he said. "I can go all night."

Oh no, I thought. I had been afraid of that.

So far, *The Year I Fucked Everybody* had always been about seeking out my own pleasure, satisfying myself. But sleeping with Viktor made me feel rudderless and out of control—I hated that feeling.

I told him I was done for the evening—I had an open call early in the morning out in Claremont. He wasn't too much of a pain about it, and eventually we both fell asleep. When I awoke I was relieved to see that he had evaporated into the desert air, and I could enjoy my morning coffee by myself and try to forget what had happened the night before.

I didn't know it at the time, but Danny Bonaduce had been right. Something had been in the air that night, something big. My one night with Viktor—so inconsequential, just a little blip in the scheme of things—lit the match on a fuse that would silently snake behind me to detonate when I least expected it, blowing a giant hole in my trajectory with the company.

That one meaningless night with Viktor would come back to haunt me.

9
≡

The Nip Slip

I was at the Factory, dropping off an expense report, when I saw it. It stopped me dead in my tracks—I recognized it right away. My old friend, my treasured heirloom.

My mom's hat.

But done over in cranberry, not black like the original. It was resting on the head of a girl wearing a turtleneck dress and red lipstick, a froth of red hair sneaking out below its brim.

It was thrilling to see it in the wild—I didn't realize they were in stores already. I wondered what other colorways they came in, who else might be wearing them around already. I must have stared too long, because the girl seemed to feel it. When she turned around, her eyes widened with a jolt of recognition.

"It's you!" she said, pointing at me. "I *know* you."

I had never seen this girl before. She spoke with a heavy accent, and I was sure I didn't know any French girls.

"I think you're confusing me with someone else," I said.

"No," she insisted. "It's you."

"Lilou, you know Kate?" Ivy asked.

I had been so gobsmacked by the hat, I hadn't even seen her there, guiding the French girl by the elbow down the same hallway she had guided me during my first trip to the Factory. It was only ten months ago, but it may as well have been a different lifetime.

"You're the girl in the video," Lilou said. "You dance."

She wagged her hips back and forth in demonstration.

When she did that little dance, a memory ignited—a night when we had to stay late and snap size rings on all the new metal hangers, back at the Sunset store when I was still a shopgirl.

The girls and I had been goofing around, mugging for Ivy's video camera while we worked. I discovered the plastic bags of size rings rattled like little percussive gourds, and I shook them to the beat as we danced to the title track from the 1968 soundtrack to *Barbarella*, which was blasting from the store iPod.

Barbarella psychedella . . .
Dazzle me with rainbow colors
Fade away the duller shade of living
Get me up hiiiiigh

We were doing our best approximation of go-go dancing, just being silly. I never gave the footage a second thought.

But Lilou, here to get fully indoctrinated at the Factory before heading back to Paris to open more stores, told me that the video of me dancing was blown up larger than life and playing in a loop in the window of the Paris American Apparel, just a few blocks from the Pompidou Center.

"Paris loves you," Lilou told me, shaking her head in amazement. "Paris just *loves* you."

Lilou was looking at me like I was something special. A celebrity. Just the way I was probably looking at Caralee when she walked off the back cover of the *LA Weekly* and into the Echo Park store the day we met.

Suddenly I began to *feel* very special—somehow a video of me had made it all the way to Paris before I had. And even better—*Paris loved me!*

That famous feeling glowed under me all day, but when I got home and bragged about it to my roommate, he was unimpressed.

"Did they pay you for that?" he asked.

"Well, I was on the clock," I said.

"That's it?" he asked.

That's it, I thought. $10.50 an hour.

"So they're using your image—without your permission—and didn't even pay you for it," he said, smugly. "They're *ripping you off.*"

I felt myself bristle at the suggestion. Anyone attacking American Apparel back then—from an old classmate at Bryn Mawr who said she was *sure* I had to be sleeping with Dov, or the two ex-employees who had just filed sexual harassment lawsuits, claiming the environment of American Apparel was full of sexual *innuendo* that created a workplace hostile to women—they were the enemy. I was in for the greater good of the company, not nickel-and-diming like some greedy Hollywood sycophant.

"You don't know what you're talking about," I said. "We're spokesmodels, we do it all." When Ivy had said that to me, it sounded inspirational, but now the words sounded hollow coming out of my own mouth. They hung in the air like misshapen clouds, hard to define.

"Sure," my roommate snorted. "Of course they want you to think that."

What a mansplaining asshole. He had *no* idea what American Apparel was really like on the inside. And he also was making huge assumptions about knowing what was best for me, which was dinging my misogyny radar. Maybe it was time to move out and get my own place now that I could afford it. I had been working so hard and it was finally starting to pay off—he was probably just jealous he was making peanuts for emptying Ben Stiller's trash can.

My roommate was a nobody—*I* was an American Apparel girl who was big in Paris.

But later that night, I couldn't get to sleep. My roommate's words were looping through my head.

You're getting ripped off. They didn't even pay you for it.

He did have a point.

Why hadn't I gotten paid for the video? Ivy hadn't even bothered to tell me that it was used for an ad campaign, or even asked me if it was all right—that felt pretty suspicious, almost dishonest. I thought we all looked out for each other here.

Here I was, modeling for the company for the simple thrill of being in the spotlight? *Please.* That wore off in about an hour. Models were supposed to make money—real money. They bought fancy cars for their mothers, they didn't get out of bed for less than ten thousand a day.

I had a brilliant idea—God, I was getting so smart and business savvy these days, I could barely stand it. I was going to go straight to a place where not only the opportunity to make some serious cash awaited me, but also some protection against getting ripped off so easily again. A place where I would be fairly compensated for the use of my image.

I just needed Elyse's help getting my foot in the door.

The door to her modeling agency, of course.

III

GLO Model Management was situated in a small office over a flower shop on Melrose Avenue, right at the intersection of Crescent Heights Boulevard. That's where the retail shops stop being eclectic and become higher end as Melrose inches toward Beverly Hills. Directly across the street was ivy-wrapped Fred Segal, where paparazzi idled curbside in their SUVs waiting for Paris or Lindsay to come out with an accordion of shopping bags under each arm. It was the era of the flannel Paul Frank pajamas, printed all over with cartoon monkeys—they were grinning vacantly at us in every color from the boutique's window.

Elyse pressed the buzzer and spoke to a garbled voice on the line. The door unlocked for us, and we climbed the stairwell to the top.

GLO specialized in short girls.

Elyse and I both topped out around the five-foot-five mark, so even in heels we were Lilliputian in the eyes of the fashion world. But it's a misconception that all models have to be of the tall, willowy variety. Maybe on the runways of Milan, but not in Hollywood, home to a vast commercial advertising industry where small girls are needed to make the men, the cars, the burgers look bigger on camera.

Elyse had been with GLO for a year and had started booking big gigs that summer. In June, she'd shot a television commercial for Levi's, jumping off the end of the Santa Monica pier in a pair of 501s. The pier was a fifty-foot fall and Elyse was deathly afraid of heights. But for a national commercial, she figured out the cost of bravery easily.

It was 30K. For that, she'd hold her breath and jump.

Thirty thousand dollars for a single afternoon of work! The sum was mind-boggling to me. Booking just one job like that would turn Los Angeles into my home, and not a place I stayed for a year or two before having to give up the dream and move back.

When I thought back to telling Ivy that I was a *feminist*, not a model, like a woman couldn't be both of those things at once, I cringed. I had gone full circle and ended up on the stodgy side of old-white-lady feminism—decreeing what a woman should and shouldn't do with her body to be respected. I was way more worldly now after seeing how American Apparel worked. There could be power in being a sex object, clearly, and there were ways to harness it to my benefit. A woman can only truly be independent when she makes her own money—and as long as I was under Dov's company thumb, I belonged to him, even down to my very own image. Feminism was about belonging to yourself. Was that Bryn Mawr, whispering in my ear? It was good to hear that voice again. When had I started tuning her out?

And most importantly—modeling was *easy*. Paris loved me and I hadn't even had to try, so imagine the fortune I could accumulate if I set my mind to it. Might as well give it a shot now. I was only twenty-four—I had the rest of my life to do important, ugly things.

III

There wasn't much to the offices of GLO.

On the wall were three floating shelves, filled with the composite cards of smiling, skinny girls of every variety. Boyish ones in motorcycle jackets, sun-fried blondes in bikinis, manic pixie dream girls with pastel shags. Clean-cut girls clutching tennis rackets, desperate-looking naked girls smeared in a greasy substance. There was Elyse with a smoky eye looking back at us.

I wondered exactly where I would fit on that wall.

The agents, Sharon and Linda, sat at two desks butting up to one another, which was a good representation of their dynamic. Sharon was a hard-boiled Brooklyn type, as blunt as her bob. Linda was a Topanga Canyon hippie in a dip-dye skirt with tinkling bells on the drawstring. They had a mean mom/nice mom vibe going, which seemed to be an effective way to conduct the business of managing girls who get their picture taken.

I watched them operate as we waited for their attention.

"You were a no-call, no-show to the Wet n Wild casting, Anna!" Sharon shrieked into the phone at some unfortunate model who had missed her call time. "If it happens again, we're not going to send you out anymore."

Then Linda clicked over on her extension to smooth things over.

"Anna-banana, the Prada store opening on Rodeo is having a party and needs some beauties—want an invite?"

It was a delicate ebb and flow, a catwalk made of eggshells, and the two of them had mastered it.

"Who do we have here?" Sharon asked, turning toward me and

Elyse. She stood up and slid her bifocals down her nose, scanning me from head to foot.

I was getting used to this, the business of being judged and judging others. I was no stranger to sussing girls out immediately and reducing them to whatever could be caught in the square of a Polaroid. It felt apropos to be on the other end—a taste of my own medicine.

"You two look just like twins," Sharon said.

Elyse and I side-eyed each other, smizing. We looked nothing alike.

Elyse was a classic beauty—a Filipina American Audrey Hepburn, bird-bone thin. I was a pretty girl you might find in a soda commercial. But we did have the same body type, the same wavy hair down our backs, and that made us the same kind of girl to Sharon. Once at the shop, Elyse's mom had confused the two of us from behind and pinched my butt instead. I had fooled her mother, and now I was fooling her agent, too.

I straightened my shoulders and stretched out my spine, trying to stand as tall as possible as Sharon squinted at me.

"What are you, a size zero? Such a tiny thing."

At American Apparel, I was always hearing that I was too skinny. How strange to be back in the real world again with the same beauty standards I thought we were transforming single-handedly. Nope. Out there in the real world, everyone was still playing the same old toxic game. But then I remembered—I was here to play the game, too, and win. Now it was *my* turn to profit off my body, and then, once I had a nice little cache of money squirreled away, I could deal with the philosophical concerns later. I had bigger fish to fry at the moment than upholding my feminist principles.

"Sometimes double zero," I told Sharon, shrugging.

Her eyes sparkled. It was music to her old-school ears.

She guided me over to a little wood-paneled nook in the back corner of the office that looked like the porny background of a 1990s Calvin Klein ad. Everything was starting to feel a little outdated at GLO.

She snapped a few pictures with a Polaroid camera—I was wearing my brother's old Devo shirt, a raglan tee I'd cut the sleeves off—and it was when we were waiting for the shots to develop that I realized I was officially in. There would be no contract, nothing for me to sign. The Polaroid was my bond—I knew from my own scouts that I'd never waste the film on anyone but a sure thing.

I let the accomplishment surge through me like an electric charge. I was one step closer to my goal, and feeling very Zen about my accomplishment. On the drive over, Elyse had been amping me up, telling me about a sneak preview she'd seen of this new motivational self-help documentary called *The Secret*. The mantra was simple:

See the things that you want as already yours.
Remember that you are a magnet, attracting everything
    to you.
Your thoughts are seeds, and the harvest you reap will depend on
    the seeds you plant.

It seemed like hokey optimism to me. *The Secret* was just the power of positive thinking, but patchouli scented. A sort of millennium manifest destiny that would go on to be a monster of its own making—launching shadowy start-ups, blinding well-meaning investors, winning presidential campaigns.

But for now, I'd try it on for size.

I had willed myself to be a GLO girl, and now I was.

I'd wanted to book some real, professional jobs, and now I *would*.

I could get into this California New Age vibe. Look how well it was working already, and I was just getting started.

I paid—no, invested—seventy-five dollars of my own money for a stack of a hundred New Faces cards from Sir Speedy print shop on Sunset. My comp card was just an eight-by-five-inch of cardstock, the

Polaroid of me in the Devo tee on the front, footnoted with the agency logo and a list of all my vitals.

Height ("5'6 ½," Sharon exaggerated), weight ("100 lbs," all Sharon), eye color ("green"—mine were brown), and hair color ("dark brown"—some truth, finally). There was also my dress size (a size smaller), bra size (a cup size bigger), and shoe size.

When I brought the cards back to GLO, Sharon handed half of them back to me and explained I'd take them to my auditions and use them as a calling card until I got more photographs together for a Look Book. Then she placed the other half of the stack on the floating shelves, where I'd live with the other GLO girls.

I decided that each time I'd visit, I'd move my card to the middle of the shelf, a place of prominence where I could be spotted easily and be the first girl on Sharon's mind at the start of every morning when requests were coming in.

What entrepreneurial gumption I had, now that I was marketing myself as a product.

But every time I'd come by, I'd find my face shuffled to the edge by the hands of the other girls, nimble with their own ambition. They'd file their face smack dab in the sweet spot, and I'd get moved over a slot. And then when the next girl came in, she'd shuffle me down even farther, and the cycle would start anew.

III

It was only a few weeks before I booked my first job. And it was a big one, or so it seemed. I had been cast as the principal girl in a music video for . . . the Rolling Stones.

The Stones!

As iconic, recognizable, and ancient as the Great Pyramids. They were classic rock idols, the biggest of them all. Anyone more legendary was already dead. Booking this job was so much cooler than a fast-food commercial, so much bigger than jumping off the pier in a pair of Levi's. And it was definitely a thousand times better than bopping around some low-res video in the Paris store for free. Modeling for the Stones made modeling for American Apparel feel as budget as a fashion show at the mall. Booking this job was the perfect way to kick things off at GLO and show them my true value. Look how I could pin down something so . . . *epic*.

I *Secreted* myself to death in the days following the audition, envisioning myself in the role—though I wasn't sure exactly what it would entail. At the audition, they handed out sticks of Dentyne and I had to kiss a friendly boy model—a jockish type right out of an underwear ad, with a shaved head and muscles rippling under a tight tee—not exactly my type, but this was acting, right? I better get used to it.

I kissed him over and over again while the casting director shouted a range of confounding instructions. *You're kissing at the movies, and you get caught by an usher! You're kissing in the woods, and you hear a bear!* As I kissed my partner, I ran my fingers up the nape of his neck and felt goose bumps there—it was working! This acting thing was going to be a breeze.

On the drive home, I asked the Universe to come through for me. I *needed* this job, Universe. When I was brushing my teeth, I asked the Universe. In line at Trader Joe's, I asked the Universe. Before I went to sleep, I asked the Universe.

A few days later, the Universe came through.

When Sharon called and told me I booked the job, I braced myself for the rate. The Rolling Stones were so huge, I knew the rate had to be, too.

"Let's see," she said. "Looks like . . ."

I held my breath.

"Two hundred and fifty," Sharon said.

"An hour?" I asked.

"A day. Less our commission, of course—twenty percent."

Hmm. Not quite what I expected.

"Oh sorry, hold on . . ."

I heard a rustle of papers on the other end of the line, and saw a glimmer of hope. Of course that low rate had to be a mistake. *$200 bucks in my pocket for the Stones?*

"They'd give you five hundred if you kiss a girl."

Oh. I guess that was a little better?

I thought it over.

Five hundred dollars for a single day's work was nothing to be a brat about. And kissing a girl for twice as much was kind of a no-brainer. I was an old pro by now—more comfortable kissing Caralee and Gia in the tub than I'd felt kissing that mystery man at the audition.

"Count me in," I told Sharon. I wrote down the shoot date—October 21, 2005—in my planner and prepared to become famous.

The video for "Rain Fall Down," a single from the Stones' twenty-fourth album, *A Bigger Bang*, was shot in an abandoned office building in downtown LA that had a looming date with the wrecking ball. It was dark and spooky inside—all the electricity had been turned off long ago. Generators hummed in a stairwell to power the set lights and equipment, and we were given flashlights to navigate the set.

My first stop was the wardrobe trailer, an RV stuffed with rolling racks of glittering vintage rockerwear. I spotted a hanger with my New Faces card dangling from it—on it was a floral brocade vest in royal purple from that complex era of 1960s fashion that can best be described as Psychedelic Renaissance Faire. The vest was Medieval Times on top—brocade with gold trim and sheer bishops' sleeves, but all 1960s sexual lib on the bottom—groovy Tina Turner fringe swishing to my knees. I'd be wearing it over a pair of my own hot shorts and a little purple bralette, two items the wardrobe lady had plucked from the bag of underwear I had brought along, like Sharon had instructed. I could think of only one other career where you carry your underwear around in a bag with you, but put it out of my mind.

I had accidentally worn my own ring to set, a small oval of turquoise on a silver band, but the wardrobe lady said that it matched my outfit, and they could use that, too. Just as I was ready to head to hair and makeup, my costar walked into the trailer.

Luna looked like a model.

She was from a big Hollywood agency for tall girls who walked runway and dated professional athletes, and she took one look at my New Faces card and my five-foot-five frame and extended her hand like she expected me to kiss it.

There wasn't going to be any getting to know each other, no pre-shoot sororal bonding. Luna strapped on a pair of headphones and scrolled through her iPod silently, only unplugging once to tell me she had gotten paid far more than the $500 day rate I was earning.

Great.

As I tugged on a pair of space-age silver platform boots, I felt a heavy ball of dread rolling around my stomach. This was not going to be easy—nothing like kissing Gia and Caralee in the tub, where we were equals and friends. Luna wanted me to know she existed in a slot far ahead of me in the modeling hierarchy, something the audition and its directives hadn't prepared me for.

You're kissing a top model who thinks she's more valuable than you. You're kissing a girl who has written you off as an amateur.

I thought about the girls who showed up to open interviews at American Apparel who weren't wearing the right outfit or didn't have the right style. I wondered if I ever made them feel this way—discounting them before they had even had a chance to prove themselves. Perhaps this was my punishment, a taste of my own handiwork. Was there some element of karmic retribution to *The Secret*?

I toddled to the hair and makeup trailer in my go-go boots behind Luna, where a team of women got busy doing things to my face that I didn't know needed fixing—trimming my eyebrows, darkening a mole on my cheek with a pencil. The stylists transformed my hair from an unruly bush to a luxurious waterfall of curls that fell steaming off their irons. At the last minute, they wrapped a silver headband across my forehead, and then it was time to head to set.

I caught a glimpse in the mirror on my way out. I looked like an extra from *Barbarella*.

The premise of our scene was that Luna and I would be kissing in a grungy bathroom stall, and then that mysterious, titular Rain Fall would shower down upon us, and we'd be so enveloped in passion, we'd barely even notice. We'd just continue kissing right through the storm.

The director of the video was Jonas Åkerlund, a black metal drummer turned directing visionary, who looked at home in the darkened cave of the building where we were shooting. He was wearing a complicated pair of engineer's boots, his face obscured by a mess of black hair. He communicated with his crew solely in Swedish—a disorienting, evil-sounding language I couldn't make any sense out of. All the words sounded like ice cracking.

He got right down to business and filed Luna and me into position— straddling a toilet. Modeling sure was proving to be a glamorous industry. A camera assistant explained that the first few takes would be just us kissing, and then they'd hit us with the water. The important thing was to ignore the water, and just keep kissing. No matter how hard it "rained," just keep kissing.

Got it, I thought. Not exactly material to be considered by the Academy, but I could handle it.

I looked over at Luna. She wouldn't even meet my eyes. How exactly was this going to work?

Åkerlund lifted an arm in the air.

"Aktion!"

I closed my eyes and leaned in and kissed Luna softly on her lips. It was like trying to romance a statue. I opened one eye a crack and took a look at her. For all the experience she had alluded to having just a few minutes earlier, it seemed like Luna was frozen with a case of the show-time nerves.

She was staring up at the lights, mesmerized. Oblivious to the whole shoot unfolding around her. Suddenly a memory floated up—so out of place here in the glamour of the shoot, I wanted to laugh.

Once at my sister's house in the country, I had been tasked with locking up the chickens for the night, only I waited too long. Night had fallen, and one had gotten left behind outside the pen, stuck in some sort of nocturnal trance. It was clearly alive—its eyes were rolling around and it was making chicken noises, but no matter how I tried to shuttle it into the barn, it wouldn't move from its spot. It was like it was nailed to the ground.

"Chickens become stupefied when they fall asleep," my sister told me. "They're awake, but off in another dimension."

I looked at Luna. It was time to make out with the stupefied chicken.

I tried kissing the expanse of her neck. Luna stayed emotionless as I ran my mouth up and down it like a corncob. After a few takes of that, Åkerlund seemed satisfied.

Now it was time for the rainfall part.

"*Spruta!*" he ordered.

A frigid spray of water hit me in the midsection, soaking my costume and sucking all the breath out of my lungs. I was spluttering through the take, trying to just *keep on kissing* Luna's chicken neck while also trying to get enough air in my lungs to survive.

Where was this powerful stream of water coming from? I shielded my eyes and found the source—a grinning Swedish man crouched below the camera, a hose clenched under his armpit. He was aiming straight for my face now, laughing as the spray soaked the perfect cascade of curls the stylist had spent the past hour working on.

What a little bastard, I thought. I'd like to show him what to do with that hose. Couldn't he see that I couldn't breathe? What was so funny about that?

"*Spruta, hårdare!*"

I braced myself.

The jettison of icy water shot through the air again, but this time strong as a fire hose. It blasted the silver headband clear off my head and my boots immediately filled up with water and split at the seams, the forty-year-old-glue dissolving in the deluge. In just a few more takes, the spray had blown all my clothes clean off, and they lay in a waterlogged velvet heap on the floor beneath me. I was just in my own underwear now.

The freezing water covered my face like a sheet. I looked over at Luna, who had suddenly squawked to life, awakened by the icy spray just like a real chicken.

"Luna," I hissed.

Her eyes finally met mine, and I offered up a plan.

"Here's how we're going to do this. On this take, you kiss me. And *I'll* breathe."

I thought it best that I go first, like a mother putting on her oxygen mask first on a crashing airplane. Once I was safe, I could worry about her.

"And then on the next take, *you* breathe, and *I'll* kiss," I said.

Luna nodded. She finally had woken up.

From that point on, everything changed. Luna and I were on the same team now, since our lives basically depended on each other. We took turns kissing and breathing, and by the time the shoot was almost through, the experience had bonded us like soldiers in a foxhole from an old-man war movie. It didn't matter who was short or tall or how much our rate was, we were in the shit together.

It was Luna and me versus the crouching Swede, hell-bent on drowning us in an icy torrent. Luna and me versus Åkerlund, who didn't speak to us in English and never asked our names. Luna and me versus the Rolling Stones, who had shot all their footage the previous day when the set would be free of extras.

Luna and me versus all the men in the room, trying to steal the very air we breathed while we played sexy. But we would prevail—we just needed to work together, shivering in our underwear.

Finally, Åkerlund signaled that it was time for the last take. Our lips were literally turning blue, but I was going to give this last one everything I had.

One more take, I told myself. *And then it'll all be over.*

So close to a fluffy dry robe in the trailer and a seat in front of the heater. I envisioned that the water from the hose was as toasty-warm as the hot springs in Ojai. I imagined that I was having no trouble at all breathing while getting blasted in the face. I was *acting*, I reminded myself. I could ignore my temporary discomfort for the good of the whole. What was more important in the end—the mission at hand or my personal comfort? It seemed like an obvious choice.

That's when it happened.

In one fell swoop, Luna's hand, slick with water, slipped down my arm and the strap of my flimsy lace bra followed. Its strap fell off my shoulder, and my right breast broke free.

Luna gasped.

We both looked down.

There it was, under the stage lights for all to see.

Of course it was old rightie—the one always sneaking out of my bikini if I swiveled in my beach chair the wrong way, the one most likely to creep over a plunging neckline. Always hungry for the spotlight, and tonight she found her big break.

"*Tack!*" Åkerlund thundered across the set.

Everything ground to a halt.

He shielded his eyes dramatically with his hand, as if my breast were

blindingly bright, and the rest of the crew did the same. In one synchro-
nized move, they turned their backs to us. As Åkerlund dipped under
the lights, I noticed his dyed black hair had a centimeter of blond Nor-
dic roots peeping through.

Their reaction was kind of amusing to me. *Jeez, what was the big
deal?* It was just a wardrobe malfunction, not exactly Janet Jackson at
the Super Bowl. What was it about a woman's exposed nipple that made
everyone lose their minds?

Wardrobe scuttled over to tuck my titty back in. Makeup used the
opportunity to touch up everything that had washed away. And Luna
apologized profusely for the accident, but I waved her off. I wasn't
embarrassed—American Apparel had normalized nudity for me. I
saw the errant boobs of my friends all the time. Modesty was an old-
fashioned concept to me now, the politeness that strangers show each
other.

I didn't give the nip slip a second thought.

Once everything was in order, the line of Swedes turned around
and resumed their positions. The little man crouched back into position
behind the hose. Åkerlund reappeared from behind a monitor, and we
continued shooting the last, watery take. By the time we had wrapped
and I had shimmied out of what little remained of my soaking wardrobe,
the misstep was far from my mind. Just a hiccup in a day in the life of a
professional model. No biggie.

I drove home so incredibly proud of myself.

III

A month and a half later, I found the video on this new website I had
heard about called YouTube.

EXPLICIT, it warned.

I rolled my eyes. Like two girls kissing was deviant behavior. God,
this repressed society we lived in. *Puritanical tribalism*, I thought.

The video wasn't exactly high art. It's shots of the Stones performing the song on a set made to look like a dingy hotel room, interspersed with phony sex scenes pantomimed by skinny twentysomethings styled in the last gasp of 1990s heroin-chic that was still blowing through the industry like a toxic fog.

One girl had the Stones' iconic tongue patch sewed on the ass of her jeans while she bucked away atop a frail Rod Stewart look-alike in a pair of leopard-spotted bikini undies. Another couple made out in the backseat of a car while the girl made scenery-chewing O faces. I knew that all of them were getting hosed down by the little man off camera, just like Luna and I had, but their scenes were shot with warm water, not freezing cold like ours. We were the first shoot of the day, and the generators hadn't had time to warm up the tank yet.

Finally, my scenes start flashing by. First there's a glimpse of Luna, looking bored, eyes rolling. Then a shot of me, kissing her neck. I began to identify familiar things—my hot shorts, my own purple bra from my underwear bag. There was my turquoise ring in close-up as my hand stroked Luna's leg, puckered with goose bumps. It was amazing how many little things of mine they used.

And then . . . there was my breast.

My mouth dropped open as the cursor reached the end of the video and I sat in stunned silence.

I scrolled back and watched it again.

The split second that my breast had been accidentally exposed was now drawn out and eroticized in slo-mo. The shot was the climax of the whole smutty video.

A hot feeling started prickling behind my ears.

Not again.

This was just like what had happened with Paris, but worse. Everyone had acted so respectfully when it happened—it hadn't even occurred to me the footage of my nip slip would be *used*. How was that even possible?

Was I supposed to have said something during the shoot?

I began to place the blame on myself—how could I have been so green not to realize? The whole time I had been patting myself on the back about what a professional I had been—but I had just made myself easy to take advantage of. Åkerlund and the Swedes used every part of my body like any prop on set that day, and I hadn't even said a word.

Weren't there, like, laws against this?

Maybe I should have called Sharon immediately when it happened and gotten them to sign something. Elyse told me you got bank for a titty shot. Wouldn't Sharon . . .

Sharon!

An escape hatch opened in my mind, and a little rope ladder descended.

Sharon was my *agent*. If there was one person I could rely on to right this wrong, it was Sharon. She was the mean one! She'd never let anyone take advantage of a GLO girl. She was like a viper with the girls, I'd seen her in action. So when it came to an unscrupulous director, I knew Sharon would fight for me. This is why people had agents, didn't they? This is why she took 20 percent of my rate.

I called Sharon and tried to keep cool as I explained what had happened, but when I was through, all that was on the other end of the line was silence.

"What's the problem, beauty?" she said. "It's the *Stones*. And you look great."

What?

Wait—maybe she wasn't quite getting what had actually happened here. I decided to try another tactic.

"But what about your commission?" I asked. Didn't she want a bigger slice? This was her business, after all. Weren't they cheating her, too?

But there was no pit bull left in Sharon. The Stones had used a few GLO girls in the video, she explained. The implication was clear—*Don't rock the boat on this big client, beauty.* The cred was more valuable than the commission to her, and I had better not raise a fuss or risk being labeled as a troublemaker, or I would never get sent out again.

She clicked me over to Linda, who offered me a discount rate at Ken Pavés salon to smooth things over.

I slammed the phone down. This betrayal stung the worst. Did anyone have my back out here? I felt so insignificant, like such a young dummy. There was nothing professional about what had happened at the shoot—the only one acting like a professional had been me.

I needed someone to answer for this.

Someone had broken the rules here, and I wanted them to get caught. I wanted an apology, or at least an acknowledgment that something *wrong* had happened. And if Sharon wasn't going to help me, I would do it on my own.

I located the number for the production company on my pay stub— Black Dog Films—and called it myself. They passed me around until a sympathetic woman picked up and listened to my story and promised to call me back with some answers. But a week went by, and then a month, and then a year, and then a decade, and I never heard a word from her.

What was this unspoken social permission for high-profile men to lay claim to women's bodies? It seemed like the bigger they were, the more entitled they became, helping themselves to anything they wanted. Sharon's implication that I should just be quiet and be grateful for the exposure stuck like a fleck of hot pepper in the back of my throat, impossible to dislodge.

GLO was nothing more than a well-greased conveyor belt, serving us girls up one by one for $250 a day. What did "professional" even mean, anyway? Being ruthless, getting what you wanted at any cost, not following the rules? It was starting to seem that way.

Then I started thinking about American Apparel, and if we were any different. If Dov was any different. Unprofessionalism was the name of the game at the company, and I always thought that was our greatest strength—working outside of the box, doing whatever it took to succeed, bucking the system.

But Dov was just using us, too, wasn't he? I had been convinced that we were a company run by women, but it was starting to seem like we were actually a giant human pyramid, set up to support the brunt of one big man at the top.

There was nothing feminist about that. Nothing empowering. It was the oldest trick in the book. Dov had built his entire empire on the backs of women, and to make matters worse—in the cases of Caralee and Natalie and Ivy and who knows who else—sometimes they were on their backs, literally.

10

The Hypnotist

By that fall of 2005, three former employees had filed sexual harassment lawsuits against Dov. Gloria Allred represented two of them.
The girls—a former store manager, a customer service rep, and a scout—
weren't claiming that Dov had pressured them for sex. By their own
account, he never slept with any of them. Instead they were alleging that
the corporate workplace was *intimidating* to women, with its vintage
Hustlers and *Playboys* decorating the stores. There was too much talk of
vibrators, of masturbation—*sexual misconduct*. One plaintiff said Dov
paraded around in his American Apparel briefs at the store and invited her
to masturbate with him. The girls had been damaged by Dov's *egregious*
expressions of sexual freedom, and now they wanted to be compensated.

My suspicions were starting to grow about the validity of Dov's
contemporary male brand of millennial feminism, but was he a *sexual
harasser*? I read an article in the *New York Times* about the lawsuits, and
I thought the claims of the girls sounded pretty patronizingly offensive.
They made us out to be shrinking violets who needed to be politely
protected from the evils of pornography, instead of grown women with
our own sexual agency. That brand of goody-goody Dworkin feminism

seemed so infantilizing to me. One of the lawsuits even cited *crude language*.

Dov considered them a timely cash grab now that the company was pulling in a couple hundred million a year, and I could see it that way, too.

If you're seasick, don't join the navy.

It was a quote from one of Dov's supporters in the *Times* article, and I understood that, too. This is the fashion business—a creative field full of passionate outsider weirdos who push boundaries. Unorthodoxy was the lay of the land, and that's why I loved working in the industry so much. If someone doesn't want to make a living in a provocative environment, there's always a job at the library.

Plus, I had never seen Dov harass anyone. He never harassed me? All the girlfriends I knew were willing participants—it didn't seem like anyone was getting abused here. But the claim about Dov wearing only his underwear to work and asking an employee to masturbate with him? That kind of did *seem* like the very definition of sexual harassment, I had to admit.

With the *Jane* reporter, it had been easy for me to write off the whole thing as a mutually beneficial, consensual arrangement. But an unwilling employee who needed the paycheck? I couldn't ignore the creepiness. That one was much harder to explain away.

There was one other thing that jumped out at me from the article. One of the girls had been a scout, and she had filed her lawsuit in July, not long before I locked down the position. Did I get the gig because I had *vision*, or was there just an opening for someone placid enough to not make a fuss when she walked in on the big boss in the dressing room with Caralee? Did I get rewarded because I had pretended it was no big deal to me? Was earning my precious job really just another hollow achievement—a Cracker Jack prize instead of the diamond I thought I'd polished up for myself?

I couldn't let myself think that. I was a good scout, responsible for bringing in scores of hardworking *lifers* just like me. I'd earned my job, and those lawsuit girls were just grifters, taking advantage of Dov. He was so honest about everything, it made him an easy mark. It didn't take long to convince myself of that.

III

One afternoon in early November, I was finishing up an open call at the Sunset store when Dov's champagne-colored Caddy pulled up outside.

"He's here!" Anarah yelled.

She sounded the alarm, and it ricocheted through the shop.

It's DOV! Look busy! Toss any food—no drinks on the cash wrap! Exterminate all dust bunnies. Cover all exposed tattoos. One last quick mirror check for fuckability before he—shit, he's here!

"Everyone!" Dov barked, throwing open the shop doors. "Back room meeting."

He stormed the floor like a gale-force wind, hangers rattling in his wake, and disappeared into the back.

The door opened again and belched out a backstock boy.

"He told me to man the cash wrap, but I've never done that before," he said, panicking.

"Figure it out," I ordered, before heading back myself.

Something was up.

III

Dov was jubilant.

One of the lawsuits had been dropped that afternoon. A federal district court judge had dismissed the case and entered an order that American Apparel pay nothing to the plaintiff. Dov gathered us all into the back room of his precious baby of a first store to celebrate.

"A defeat against conservatism cloaked as liberalism," he yelled, shaking a fist in the air. He was buzzing around the back room, smiling manically at us.

Dawn, Gia, Anarah—all the girls were standing at attention. I spotted Big Dick Vik unloading a box of 2001s. He winked at me. We hadn't spoken since our date at Star Shoes, but I'd heard through the backstock boy grapevine that he had been bragging about our night of underwhelming sex. I rolled my eyes at him and looked back to Dov.

He was holding up his hand for high fives and dancing like he'd scored a touchdown.

"Have you read *The 48 Laws of Power*?" he asked one of the boys. "I'll get you a copy. Law number two—Never put too much trust in friends. Let's take these suits for what they really are—PC bullshit. We're changing culture here, and it's big work. There are puritanical forces set to destroy everything we've built so far! *Don't let them.*"

There was that us-versus-them dynamic again—all of us, together, unified in purpose against an unseen enemy. It was easy to get swept up in—Dov's charisma. He had *won*, and by default, we were all winners now. I started clapping for him along with the others.

I looked over at Dawn. She was clapping, too, transfixed.

"Now listen," he said, propping a foot on a stool. "When you're successful, you attract hangers. Laggers."

A switch flicked inside him, and his eyes darkened.

"Opportunists!" he snarled. He punched the desk, and a stack of paperwork kited to the ground. Anarah scrabbled to pick them up.

The back room went silent—he had swapped euphoria for blind rage so quickly, no one was sure how to react. I could hear the thud of the store iPod pumping through the drywall, chugging along while he recalibrated. We made eye contact, and his glare softened a bit. He ran a hand through his hair and took a deep breath.

He was quiet for a minute while we shifted uneasily in our spots—he

May Day at Bryn Mawr, my feminist utopia of a Seven Sister college

Come join our team, the card read. I took it
from her hand immediately.

The Factory was a hulking warehouse painted millennial pink.

I was a real-deal American Apparel girl now.

It was a classic black felt floppy with white contrast stitching along the band.

I could get down with being a spokesmodel, as long as it came with a regular paycheck.

OBEY YOUR MASTER-

BAITER

I WILL!

Was it a pun, or just an activist without a spell-check?

All my time on and off the clock was spent with employees—my new family.

On Saturdays, we'd wear roller skates while we worked,
one collision away from a lawsuit.

Sometimes we'd drag a kiddie pool outside and splash around in our bikinis.

Even at Bryn Mawr, it turns out that the male gaze is too strong to appropriate.

I typed the destination of the Boston store—330 Newbury Street—into my TomTom. I figured I'd get started there.

The Nextel had a walkie-talkie function, so now I was never truly alone.

KATE

But then I remembered—I was here
to play the game, too, and win.

I had willed myself to be a GLO girl,
and now I was.

I floated along, paycheck to paycheck,
anesthetized by the pleasures of Los Angeles.

I rolled to Philly for the store opening there.

That was the beginning of the end—stores started
opening in malls.

California—a chaotic fantasyland where everyone was young
and no one wore biz-cas.

I couldn't help but feel crushed, seeing our utopia falling.

seemed to sense that he scared us. Suddenly he leaped to his feet and jerked his jogging pants down to the ground. Underneath was a pair of pink American Apparel briefs, the ones with the white piping.

The backroom erupted in laughter.

I laughed, too, grateful for a break in the heaviness. The tension hanging in the air started to dissolve, and soon we were all on the same team again. All winners here.

My eyes ran over the hairy expanse of Dov's thighs and settled on the bulge in his underwear. It struck me as kind of profound that whatever was covered there by a few cubic inches of American-made cotton could be the root of so much turmoil. Truly the crotch that launched a thousand ships.

It was the driving force propelling all this provocative chaos that was making the company thrive. It could cause a press frenzy, could launch an empire, could even destroy it.

"Anyone offended by this?" he asked, shuffling across the room, his pants around his ankles.

He looked ridiculous. We were all eating it up—now it was really a party.

"Are you offended?" he said, pointing to Gia. She was fanning away the tears in her eyes from laughing so much.

"Nope," Gia said.

"How about you?" he asked Dawn.

"No way!" she yelled.

"You?" he said to Viktor.

"Fuck no."

"What about you?" he said, pointing at me.

I shook my head no.

"Good. This is a big win for all of us—for all of you."

He gathered us together in a huddle.

"Fuck sexual harassment culture! It's the fabrication of a bunch of pierced protestors. It makes victims out of women, and if there's one thing I can't stand, it's victim culture. Don't fall for it."

A buzz from his phone distracted him.

"I gotta take this. Go and spread the word," he told us, hitching up his pants.

We were still clapping and high-fiving each other when the Caddy pulled back out onto Sunset Boulevard. It had only taken a few minutes to whip us all into a frenzy, but it stayed with everyone the rest of the afternoon. *American Apparel versus the world!*

Bonnies and Clyde, that was us.

III

How did I get so hypnotized?

How did I get to a place where I was actually applauding a man with multiple sexual harassment lawsuits pending against him? How did I find myself on the side *opposing* Gloria Allred, the most famous feminist attorney of all time?

It had all happened so quickly, I hadn't realized how deep I was falling. But that's what hypnotists do. They disconnect you from your own self-consciousness, weakening the connections between you and the outside world you've always known. They make you do things you would never consider in your normal life.

I'll never forget the first time I saw one in action.

I had just arrived at Bryn Mawr—those isolating first days on campus where all the girls are strangers. The hypnotist was administration-prescribed entertainment for the freshwomen to break the ice and get to know each other, and it was the only event on the corny list of a cappella concerts and stand-up comedians that interested me. I had been looking forward to it all week.

I was sure hypnotism was all one big illusion and that I could *never* be hypnotized. I knew myself too well by then—I was too type A, too caffeinated, too hyperaware of my surroundings at all times for a crystal to be swung in front of my eyes and suddenly I'm *getting very sleepy*? Impossible.

I was sitting in the front row when the red velvet curtains parted and an old man in a burgundy suit stepped out, holding a skinny Bob Barker microphone. His hair had an unnatural weft to it—a toupee! *Ha.* I can spot one gleefully from a mile away. This hypnotist was definitely not going to pull one over on me.

"Hello, ladies," he said. "Are you prepared to be under my control?"

The crowd tittered nervously. Onstage behind him sat a row of empty chairs.

"Who doesn't believe that hypnotism is real?" he asked.

A few hands shot up right away. I raised mine, too.

Ooh pick me, I thought. Let me up there where I could see all the trickery up close, rip off the metaphorical toupee of falsity, and expose this sham once and for all. I eyed the chosen girls enviously as they filed onstage and took their seats.

The hypnotist paced behind them like a tiger at the zoo.

"Do you think I can hypnotize you?" he asked, leaning over the first girl.

"No," she said. Her voice was strong.

"Oh?" the hypnotist said, twiddling his fingers mischievously. "I say you're hypnotized *right now.*"

He reached out and snapped his fingers, and the girl instantly crumpled onto the shoulder of her neighbor, in a deep sleep. A gasp ran through the crowd.

"Oh, would you look at that?" The hypnotist gave us an expression of mock shock.

The girl she rested on looked back at us in fear, because she knew she was next.

"What about you?" he asked. "Do you think you're hypnotized right now?"

"I don't *think* so," she said. But when the hypnotist snapped, her body bent like a hinge, too, and her head came to rest right in the crotch of the first hypnotized girl. A wave of laughter coursed through the room, but neither girl moved.

I had to admit it all *seemed* real, but maybe all these girls were plants, hired by the hypnotist to sell the illusion. I recognized one of them, though—Tess, who lived in the smoking dorm and lunched in the vegetarian dining hall and had one gray eye like David Bowie. She seemed like the very definition of cool composure. But when the hypnotist snapped, she crumpled, too.

He gestured at the row of wilted girls.

"Now, all these young women are under a great and powerful spell."

He rubbed his hands together.

"So let's have some real fun."

Overhead there was the popping of speakers, and a voice crackled down from the rafters:

"Ladies and gentlemen, this is . . .

I recoiled in horror as a techno horn began to toot above our heads.

. . . Mambo Number Five!"

"Does anyone feel like *dancing*?" the hypnotist asked, his face corrupted by an evil smile.

He extended his palm over the chairs of the sleeping girls, and they all began to stir in their seats while the song blared,

A little bit of Monica in my life
A little bit of Erica by my side
A little bit of Rita's all I need
A little bit of Tina's what I see.

No! I wanted to stop him, but it was too late—the girls were all doing dorky mom dances to the canned track. The formerly cool Tess was now aggressively executing a version of the Roger Rabbit. Did she even know what she was doing? She'd never live this one down.

The hypnotist snapped his fingers, and the track silenced. The girls blinked back to life, blessedly unaware of how far into the abyss of degradation they had just plumbed. He dispatched each of them from the stage until only one girl remained.

For his last trick, he told her that she had won the lottery.

The girl jumped up and down, screaming in ecstasy, before he cut her off.

"Oh no, wait just a minute," he said, scratching at his toupee like he was greatly confused. "There has been a terrible mistake."

There had been some problem with the numbers, he explained.

"You *didn't* win the lottery, my dear," he told her.

The girl's eyes began to well with tears, and a loud wail emerged from deep inside her. It filled up the entire auditorium until even the hypnotist seemed startled, and he tried snapping her back to life.

"You're awake!" he said.

But the girl kept wailing, inconsolable over the loss of her fortune.

"Aaaand you're awake!" he ordered.

He snapped again and again, but the girl wouldn't budge from her trance. A good Samaritan from her dorm got onstage and pulled her back to her seat, and it seemed like all was well for a while. But just as he was wrapping things up, a pained yelp rang out from the back of the auditorium again.

It was the hypnotized girl. She couldn't seem to get *un*hypnotized.

"You're AWAKE!" he yelled at her, snapping frantically. "YOU'RE OUT OF IT!"

But the girl stayed under his command. When we filtered out of the auditorium at the end of the show, I saw her waiting in the lobby for him, chaperoned by a nervous-looking RA.

Still hypnotized.

After that night, anytime I would see that girl on campus, I'd think, *There's that poor girl who couldn't get unhypnotized.* And every time our paths crossed, I'd wonder how could someone fall in so deep? How could the phony promises of the hypnotist blend so inexorably with the real world that the girl couldn't tell them apart? Could someone really take control over you just like that?

Hypnotism *was* real.

It was scary to watch someone get so deep into something that they couldn't find their own way out.

11

The Big House

In the fall of 2005, I hit one year in LA.

I celebrated by signing the lease on my very own apartment—an attic studio in a hundred-year-old house that had been carved into apartments in Frogtown, a tiny neighborhood underneath a nesting of freeway interchanges next to the Los Angeles River. It was a surprisingly natural enclave. The concrete chute of the river has a natural bottom there, and it was full of shaggy blue heron diving for fish and toads that sang all night. I never realized a city like Los Angeles could be so pastoral.

Off to the west was Forest Lawn cemetery, planted full of dead film stars from Hollywood's Golden Age to watch over me. At night, a big electric crucifix atop the church there sent a beam of light to bounce around my dark kitchen like a persistent mote of glitter.

It was my first time living alone, and I loved it. I ignored all the initial drawbacks—the 5 freeway was so close there was a permanent rattle in my apartment, so it was like sharing the place with a poltergeist. But at night, the hum of the traffic was a white-noise lullaby—I thought of all the people coming and going on their own cosmic Californian journeys, and it brought me comfort as I'd drift off to sleep. Even though I was so far from home, I wasn't really alone. And once I was settled, I adopted a kitten and named her Squeaky Fromme, after the least culpable Manson girl.

My attic rose higher than all my neighbors' rooftops and gave me a spectacular view of my new neighborhood. Right across the river lay the Technicolor scrim of the San Gabriel mountain range—it had a cinematic quality, changing with the light of the day. In the morning, it reflected pink. At night, a psychedelic purple doom flickered in. So different from the relentless green of Pennsylvania. Watching sunsets through the skylight became a hypnotic experience—I was transfixed by all the new beauty.

It was cheap for a studio, but expensive for me—$750 a month and worth every penny. Just a few months ago, living in a company apartment full-time would have been something aspirational to me, but I was starting to realize that free rent was a Dov girl thing. A cost of its own. Having my own apartment meant having access to a neutral territory where I could think, a place to be truly independent. I wouldn't be compromising too much of myself if I stayed here, where I could watch all the craziness from a safe distance.

As long as I paid for my own place, I'd be okay.

I had to be sure to never lose it.

III

Soon Dov moved into a new place, too. It was a major upgrade from the thousand-square-foot Echo Park bungalow he'd been calling home for the past three years while he built the company from scratch. The working-class kid from Canada swapped the humble digs for his own Playboy Mansion in the Silver Lake hills—a four-million-dollar safe haven where he could keep a watchful eye on the US Bank tower blinking from the downtown skyline.

All the girls called it the Big House.

It was a great big Deco mansion on Apex Avenue, all of Los Angeles hanging around it like a diorama. A palatial bunker of sorts, it was built a hundred years ago by another eccentric business tycoon named Frank Garbutt, who designed the house to be a concrete fortress because of his debilitating phobia of earthquakes.

"An unshakable house," the paranoid Garbutt decreed, so the walls, the floors, and even the roof were constructed of concrete and lined in fireproof travertine. Each door was reinforced with steel. There were no fireplaces. Tucked away in the Big House, a family could survive any Californian natural disaster, and all with a view of the Hollywood sign, which captioned the windows on its north side.

When Caralee asked me to come to dinner at the Big House, I was pumped. The purchase of the property had been big news, but invites seemed reserved for the hallowed inner circle of American Apparel employees. Now I was counted among them, too—a trip to the Big House was an acknowledgment of how far I had come, and no matter how I had been feeling about Dov lately, I was proud that I had made it that far up the ladder.

I earned my invite to the Big House and I hadn't had to fuck Dov to get it.

I was such a good little feminist.

III

Caralee was waiting for me at the foot of a huge staircase that led to the Big House's front door. It was as imposing as the steps of the Lincoln Monument, dwarfing her—she looked out of place in front of them, like a high schooler on a field trip in her Ray-Bans and jean shorts. She twisted a cigarette out underfoot and gave me a wave.

Caralee was back from Tel Aviv with a tan. I was back from Minneapolis with a cold. We hugged as though we hadn't seen each other in years.

She held out my arms and gave me the once-over.

"Did you get extensions?" she asked.

"No, my hair just got long. Did you dye yours?"

Caralee's hair had golden bits woven through it like tinsel.

"No, I learned how to surf in Tel Aviv and the sun bleached it."

After full inspection and approval of each other's appearances, we climbed the stairs to the landing in front of the door. The setting sun had produced a dreamy haze over the city with only the tops of palm trees poking through. Planes twinkled like shooting stars as they zoomed across the peachy-gold sky.

It was a glorious view of the city I was conquering.

"I'll give you the tour," Caralee said.

I followed her up the rest of the giant staircase and through the front door.

We stepped into a cavernous foyer with glossy cherrywood walls, an ornate teak ceiling, and the noble scent of old wood. The room was empty of furniture but filled with a dozen rolling racks loaded with sample garments, handwritten spec tags fluttering from each one.

I reached for a cotton bathrobe that I had never seen before.

The WIFECOAT
    Sz XS-XL, Cotton terry,
    Miguel on 4th floor dye bath:
    Salmon, lemon, ~~stone~~, pink

It was a comfy cotton robe with a Peter Pan collar that rested sweetly above a row of covered buttons. Much longer than the 1970s terry robes that grazed the midthigh, and way more demure. It looked like a vintage 1950s housecoat, something to wear rollers and flip eggs in.

So *domestic*.

The Wifecoat was an anomaly amid the sensual disco-glitz look that

American Apparel had been evolving into these days. What exactly was en vogue about being a housewife? After nine months in the company, marriage seemed like an old-fashioned concept to me, like tuberculosis. I didn't really see its commercial appeal.

"Dov's obsessed with the Wifecoat," Caralee said. "He's shooting it upstairs right now."

She gestured to a set of double doors at the top of the stairs, shut tight.

I wondered which poor dummy was getting shot in there and only compensated with a little bit of spotlight and a free iPod from Circuit City, the going rate for a sexy photoshoot with Dov.

What a rip-off, I thought. I had been stripped of all my delusions about modeling. I had played that game and lost, and now I was over it.

Sounds and good smells were emanating from the kitchen, the only room alive with activity. A lofted skylight poured sun onto Wedgwood blue tiles hand painted with vegetables alongside their French names, which seemed comically quaint as a crew of Dov girls in crop tops buzzed around a pot of chicken soup bubbling on the stove. His favorite.

I recognized two of the girls.

Aika was new in town, from a rural corner of Japan and here on a work visa. I had seen her following Dov around at the Factory, learning the ropes. Aika was older than all of us. She was in her early thirties, not that you'd be able to tell by looking at her.

Junie was a local girl, nineteen, fresh out of private school and already appearing in ad campaigns. She was devoted to Dov and the company, and even went as far as harassing one of the girls who filed a lawsuit and getting slapped with one herself. Junie was a loyal subject—one of Dov's favorites.

Aika spotted me and Caralee, and brought over two champagne flutes, each with something floating in it. The waxy-sweet smell of jasmine wafted from my glass as I took it.

I looked in and saw a single bloom of tuberose bobbing around inside, threaded with silvery champagne bubbles.

"An aphrodisiac," Aika said.

I brought the glass to my lips and took a sip. I waited to feel something.

Junie drained her glass and hovered over Aika's shoulder for a refill.

"Everyone must share," Aika told her, slapping her hand away.

Junie stomped brattily into the corner to sulk. She was always a reliable font of crabby teenage attitude, but there seemed to be something else up her ass today. She barely looked at us when we said hello and ignored Caralee's invite to join the rest of the tour.

We left her in the kitchen and continued to the dining room, Aika leading the way. Giant picture windows filtered golden light onto a long oak table set with laptops instead of plates. A row of girls I recognized from the upper Factory echelons sat typing away.

Tap tap tap tap tap tap.

There was one empty place setting at the head of the table. Aika stopped to straighten the silverware.

Daddy's seat.

How patriarchal, I thought, before I could stop myself.

"Perfect, right?" Caralee said.

"Huh?" I asked.

"The light," she clarified.

I nodded—the house was beautiful, there was no doubt about that—and I wanted to see all of it. We climbed the stairs that led to the master bedroom's set of double doors where the photoshoot was taking place.

"Who's in there?" I asked.

Caralee put a finger to her lips, and we listened for a second.

"Not Junie." She stifled a laugh. "She's so pissed. She wanted to shoot the Wifecoat."

That explained Junie's black mood. She was jealous. Something that Caralee never seemed to be.

Up until that point, I had always thought of Caralee as the ultimate sexually liberated woman, but seeing her in the Big House where everyone had to share, waiting her turn in the sisterwife rotation to get shot by Dov and then printed on the backs of *LA Weekly*s in her most intimate moments—it all struck me as very sad and exploitative.

"Wait until you see this," Caralee said, grabbing my hand, breaking my train of thought. "I have a present for you."

She led me into a boring little bathroom on the second floor and swung open the door to a small linen closet.

"Ta-*da*!" she said, gesturing wide like a showgirl.

I stared at the bounty in front of me.

The entire closet was packed with brand-new Hitachi Magic Wands. There must have been a hundred of the massager-cum-vibrators that first hit the market in 1968, tiled up to the ceiling in blue-and-white boxes.

Wow.

What little furniture there was in the Big House was midcentury, and apparently even the sex toys were vintage here. Dov's commitment to aesthetic ran deep. The Magic Wand plugged into the wall, Caralee explained. No need for batteries anymore.

"Dov got a bunch to give to the workers at the Factory for their sore shoulders, and you know, for other stuff, too," she said, laughing,

Free English lessons, fair wages, and free sex toys—a 2000s rebranding of the American Dream. As creepy as Dov could be, stunts like this were endearing to me. Being provibrator *is* being prowomen, and sometimes I had to admit he had the right idea—the stopped clock of the fashion industry.

"Here," Caralee said, shoving a box in my hand. "Take one."

I rode off on the Magic Wand that very night. I could see why it hadn't gone out of style. From then on, I always had access to a surefire way to get myself off. I used it for many years until it was so well-worn, a firebolt shot out of its fraying cord and singed my buttcheeks, and I started looking into more contemporary methods of self-pleasure.

Downstairs the chicken soup still simmered on the stove in the kitchen, the chair still empty at the head of the table, waiting for its occupant to finish shooting the Wifecoat upstairs. After two glasses of aphrodisiacal libations, I wasn't feeling anything but hunger, but it seemed like no one was going to eat until Dov came down.

Caralee took me to a second-floor balcony, where the skyline was glimmering in the dusk. We sat on the ground and watched the sun settle. It grabbed the last bits of light and pulled them under the horizon like a handful of tulle. I was starting to feel the throb of a champagne headache kicking in as Caralee started telling me about something that happened the night before.

This time it was Caralee in the master bedroom with Dov.

"We were *doing it*," she said.

It was weird, for all of Caralee's sexual experience, she always referred to the act in childish euphemism. She even referred to her vagina as her *cookie*. It was kind of unnerving. A grown woman using baby talk to describe sex with Daddy was like a generic porn plot—why couldn't she use the right words?

Caralee and Dov were *doing it* on his bed in the master bedroom when the door swung open, and someone else silently padded into the room.

"Who?" I asked.

"It was Aika!"

I thought about Aika busting in with a platter of champagne with tuberose, offering it to the two of them.

"What was she doing in there?" I asked.

"She had a bowl of ice water and a little towel," Caralee said. "And she wiped each of our foreheads, and then she left."

"Dov says Aika is his *geisha*."

A wave of nausea ebbed over me.

A *geisha*?

I tasted bitter metallic at the back of my throat. Was tuberose toxic? Had I been *poisoned*? Something was making me sick.

A voice inside me screamed that this wasn't right. It was so ugly, so *racist*. So undeniably messed up. There was nothing empowering about being some man's geisha. I knew all about the patriarchy from Bryn Mawr—but now that I was so deep in its landscape, I couldn't identify it. It had been all around me the entire time.

Caralee was still giggling about Aika the geisha, like it was just another of Dov's endearing eccentricities.

I kept my mouth shut—I didn't want to make her feel like I was judging her. She was one of my closest friends.

But a *geisha*?

That was really fucked-up.

III

"Why is it taking so long?" she wailed.

A tense silence hung in the air, Junie at its epicenter. Caralee and the rest of the girls at the table ignored her for their laptops.

Tap tap tap tap tap.

"I made the little salad he likes," Junie said, snapping her laptop shut at the dining room table.

I stared down at my empty plate.

The thrill of being one of the in crowd in the Big House had worn off. This wasn't a revolutionary egalitarian society, all of us equals. We weren't a family, looking out for one another.

We were a straight-up *harem*.

My head was spinning—I needed to get home to the safety of my apartment, as far as possible from this perverted game of house. And I had to do it before Dov came downstairs, and I was unwillingly written into another scene of piggy patriarchal role-play.

"Who is up there, anyway?" Junie demanded.

Tap tap tap tap tap tap tap tap.

Junie paced the room, mouth screwed shut. But I could read the anger in her eyes as easy as a teleprompter.

THAT FUCKING WIFECOAT!

She stormed to the kitchen and grabbed a set of keys from a hook. She tossed us one last disgusted look over her shoulder as she headed for the door. I heard her start down the giant stone staircase before the steel door swung shut and muffled her footsteps.

I could see Junie through the windows as she got into one of the company Mercedes outside. She sat at the wheel for a few minutes as still as a mannequin before starting the ignition and beginning her slow descent down the winding driveway.

I wondered where she was going. The Big House was her home now—there was nowhere else *to* go. Junie was like a child running away who would only make it to the end of the driveway. Caralee caught me watching.

"All she wants is attention," she said, dismissively. "Don't give her any."

"She's a child," Aika said. She had come back in from the kitchen with a fresh bottle of champagne for anyone who needed a refill.

I stared at Aika.

She was right. Junie was only nineteen, and very much a child, still.

It was time to leave the Big House. I doubted dinner would ever be coming for me. It was all tuberose and champagne there, as much as I wanted, but nothing real. No sustenance. I told Caralee I had a headache—which wasn't really a lie—and got myself out of there. I drove my Honda home and stopped at Jack in the Box on the way, ripping the paper like an animal, inhaling the tacos, chasing away my hangover with the holy trifecta—salt and grease and hot sauce.

I was starving for something real, but this would do the trick. Now I could think straight, and it was getting harder and harder to brush off the facts.

Things at American Apparel—the company I believed in more than I believed in myself—were seriously fucked.

I just needed to sleep. To wake up tomorrow and start over again in a work world that I controlled. I had a meeting with Ivy the next morning at the Factory to go over the pipeline of new store openings—first up was Eugene, Oregon, where I'd stay through Thanksgiving. Then I'd head to Seattle. I'd be back out traveling again, being my own boss. I could forget about Dov and the Big House and the geisha.

Just as I drifted off that night in my new apartment, a chirp on my Nextel jolted me away.

It was Caralee.

"Why did you leave so early?" She moaned. *"You missed it!"*

She said I'd never believe what happened after I left.

"Junie came back," Caralee said. "She was so mad at Dov, she totally *lost* it and drove her car up the stairs."

I tried to fit all the weird parts together.

"The *Big House* stairs?"

"Yes!" Caralee said, laughing. "Where else?"

It turned out Junie really did have nowhere to go. She tore around town aimlessly for a few hours to cool down, but nothing helped. All she could think about was that fucking Wifecoat.

"She drove the *Mercedes* up the stairs?" I asked.

"Yes!" Caralee repeated.

I envisioned the Mercedes darting up the driveway, razoring a clean path right through the hedge of delicate tea roses planted at the foot of the steps.

"How far did she make it up?" I asked.

"Pretty far! At least halfway."

Holy shit! I burst into laughter.

"Was Dov mad?"

I imagined the doors to the master bedroom flying open at long last. Dov scrambling down the stairs, balls bobbling wildly beneath a bathrobe, camera still in hand.

I laughed even harder.

"Not really," she said. "He didn't really know what to do."

I pictured Dov standing there, looking out of his element for perhaps the first time ever—unsure what to do in these uncharted territories he always claimed to navigate so easily. I pictured Aika running to assist.

"You're right, I left way too early," I said.

"You shoulda stayed," Caralee said. "I missed you."

I drifted off to sleep feeling warm, fantasizing about Junie's revenge.

That little brat had discovered a way to make Dov vulnerable in his very own fortress! I never would have expected that she'd be the one to make the Big House shake, but I was proud of her.

The Wifecoat was a dud when it hit select stores that winter. It never went into full production.

12
===

The Bridge

In Los Angeles, the autumn bleeds into winter so quickly it's hard to tell them apart. The seasons are twin sisters, and they meld together to create a monoseason that hangs around until the Santa Anas blast it out of there in January and winter truly begins. Only then is it cold enough to wear a hoodie over your tank top, but still warm enough to go skinny-dipping in somebody's pool on New Year's Eve.

I was homesick and hungry for a taste of the autumn that I had missed—the showy explosions of fall color that would streak through the Poconos, filling the air with the sweet rot of what was once fresh green summer. I missed the cold air, the hot drinks. A sky full of stars. So when I heard some of the American Apparel kids were putting feelers out for a camping trip up north to chilly Big Sur, I knew I had to go.

I needed a break from all the craziness, too—a weekend away from Los Angeles and the shadow of the Big House, Dov, and the mounting lawsuits. In early December 2005, he was interviewed on *20/20*—not to discuss the future of ethical manufacturing in America, but to defend himself and his habits of dating employees, to deny the validity of the claims in his lawsuits.

He was an infamous celebrity now, looming larger than our message—the whole world wanted to know if an ethical business could be run by an unethical man.

I wasn't so sure anymore. A camping trip in the woods was just what I needed. An opportunity to stop thinking about it, run amok in nature, and do mushrooms in the woods with the girls.

Big Sur's beauty was legendary, and I had never seen a redwood in person—they seemed so much more majestic than the pines I knew from home. The other campers would be an assortment of employees—mostly girls but a few backstockers, too—from the Los Feliz and Sunset shops. No royalty from the Big House. Just us commoners—the *real* family I always felt most comfortable with.

My girl Gia would be riding shotgun on the car ride up, and we'd share a tent at the campground. Big Dick Vik was coming, too, of course. Dov was practically petting his head during that pep rally in the back room a few months earlier, and his star had only risen higher since. Viktor was a backstock manager now—getting traveling gigs and training backstock employees at new stores across the country in his skaterboy image.

Noora and Isco, two cuties from the Los Feliz store, also threw down for the campsite—I liked Isco and had hooked up with him a few times, despite his predilection for wearing fedoras, and Noora was chill, too. She grew up in a famous house that was used in a Nicole Kidman movie, and she had a mellow demeanor gleaned from years of negotiating with nervy fans hanging around her doorstep. I knew both of them would be good mushroom-tripping companions.

But there was another camper tagging along that I wasn't so sure about.

Cyrus was a backstock boy from the Little Tokyo store, and he'd be bringing his hairstylist girlfriend, Laurel, a congenial ditz who worked at the Rudy's on Hollywood Boulevard. I knew them only as acquaintances. That Halloween, Laurel had borrowed my 1960s après-ski goat fur boots for her cavewoman costume, and then gave them a blow-out and rubbed them down with special hair oil until they looked better than they ever did before, even on the goat.

I didn't mind Laurel, but she wasn't an American Apparel employee, and it made her a bit of an outlier in the crew. I always liked it better when it was just us, no one else around who might call out the dysfunction. But there was something about Cyrus that always rubbed me the wrong way. He had a fatphobic vibe I'd clocked once when I saw him giving the size 2 Laurel a hard time for eating a Snickers bar.

"It's *unhealthy*, babe," he said, tossing it in the trash.

And equally off-putting was his habit of getting handsy when he partied.

"Hugs!" he'd cry, and go in for a grope. I hated that sleazy hat trick. Cyrus was bringing the mushrooms, though, so I'd deal.

Sometimes you have to sacrifice for the greater good of the whole.

I knew that well enough by now. It was the ethos of the company, and I could practically hear Dov's voice saying it in my head. No matter how hard I tried to leave him behind, parts of him were always with me.

III

On the afternoon of the camping trip, I picked up Gia at her place on Echo Park Ave., where we loaded up my car with all our provisions and prepared for the voyage north. We took scenic Route 1, which snaked atop the coastal cliffs that edged the Pacific Ocean, churning its aqua boil right below the highway. It was a dangerous, beautiful ride.

On the way there, I worked up the courage to ask Gia about that afternoon at Squaresville, right before our sapphic bathtub shoot. The threesome-for-Berlin exchange convo I'd overheard. I noticed Gia had never left for Berlin, so what exactly had happened there?

"Oh that," Gia said, brushing it off. "It was nothing. I don't want to move up bad enough to sleep with Dov."

"You're not sleeping with him?" I asked.

"What?" Gia said. She looked at me like I had two heads.

"He's . . . *old*," she spat out.

I stared back at her. I had always just *assumed*.

Gia seemed to catch herself and started to apologize.

"I'm sorry, I didn't mean it. He's not *that* old. It's just, I'm not really into—"

She was backpedaling, explaining away the insult like it might hurt my feelings, and that's when I realized . . .

Gia thought *I* was fucking Dov, too!

All this time each of us had been thinking the other was a Dov girl and just casually sidestepping around it. It wasn't hard to figure out why—you never really knew who was and wasn't under his spell. We both collapsed into relieved laughter when I told her the truth—another bond of solidarity between us forged. As we neared Big Sur, I was feeling closer to Gia than ever.

We were somewhere around San Luis Obispo when she told me about her plan to leave American Apparel. She was going to try for a sales job at one of those fancy boutiques on Robertson where you earn a commission on top of your salary.

"That's where you can actually make money in retail. Six figs," she said. Or maybe she'd become a flight attendant, that way she could see the world and get paid for it.

"You should come with me, they'd hire us in a second," she said. "Get to Berlin on our own."

I thought about it for a moment—leaving everything to fly off with Gia to a new life. It was tempting. But being a flight attendant was another job where you had to wear a sexy costume, and working on Robertson would be a gig licking the Louboutins of the filthy rich citizens of Beverly Hills all day. I couldn't see myself doing either of those things. They both would be a step backward from where I was now—all the good parts of my job were too fulfilling, the company's mission too important. Was I going to let one big sleaze at the top ruin my cool job? I knew I'd never find one like it again.

Leaving American Apparel seemed impossible. Maybe I really was a *lifer*.

As we turned into the campground in Big Sur, we saw Cyrus and Laurel setting up their spot right by the fire. Gia and I picked a spot closer to the edge of the woods, at the base of a massive redwood. The majestic tree shot up to the heavens, tall as a city skyscraper but ancient as a dinosaur. I was already feeling bewitched by all the new nature, and I still had the mushrooms to look forward to.

Gia and I finished blowing up our air mattress and unzipped our sleeping bags—neither of us were down for roughing it—and then headed over to join the gang at the campfire. Noora and Isco had arrived with a boombox pumping Kanye's "Gold Digger" until the batteries died and the sounds of nature took over again.

The sun went down and a chill crept in, but I fended it off with an American Apparel thermal under my wool sweater. We all gathered around the fire, which roared with the promise of a good night ahead. We ate hot dogs on foraged sticks and drank icy bottles of Modelo Especial, so we wouldn't be eating the mushrooms on an empty stomach. Isco said maybe we should wait until daylight hours so we could really trip out on all the unfiltered beauty of Big Sur.

"And like, receive maximum psychedelic enlightenment," he said.

But Cyrus disagreed, and he was a mushroom scholar venerated by all the east-side backstock boys.

"If you really want to learn the secrets of the divine mushroom, it must be done at midnight," Cyrus said, nodding his head like a wise old monk.

That was how the indigenous Mazatec people of Oaxaca took them, he explained, and that was how we better do it, too.

The sun had just gone down, and we had some time to kill. Cyrus threw out the idea that we should play a game of Truth or Dare to loosen our inhibitions before the main event.

I groaned. I thought I'd left that game behind in high school. But the night was a pitch-black envelope around us—there wasn't much else to do to entertain ourselves.

It started out innocently enough. Cyrus took the first dare.

"Give me something good," he said, swigging out of a bottle of Jack and handing it to Viktor, who took a longer swig.

"I dare you to lick . . ." Gia said.

Cyrus's eyes lit up. Guys always turn into such horndogs when there's a dare involved, I remembered how these things go.

"*Yes?*" he said.

"Um . . ." Gia looked around the circle and settled on Viktor, whose eyes were glistening already. He was toasted.

"Viktor's foot."

The group of us screamed.

Cyrus licking Viktor's disgusting skater foot was an apt penance for all the *hugs!* I'd endured, for the wasted Snickers bar. I leaned in to watch it all go down.

Viktor took off one of his etnies. His foot had a crispy sock baked onto it that looked like it hadn't been changed since Brad left Jen for Angelina.

He peeled it off, miming like a burlesque performer.

"*Bum bum da da da DUM,*" he sang, drunkenly, tossing his sock into the blackness behind him.

Cyrus, like a true deviant, leaned in and fellated his big toe, and we all screamed with revulsion and delight.

"Deepthroat a beer bottle!" he dared Gia next.

"I don't think so," Gia said, rolling her eyes.

"Come on," Cyrus whined. "If you pick dare, you *have* to do it."

"Noora," he said. "French-kiss Kate."

"Mmm, why don't you kiss Vik?" she countered.

Cyrus brushed her off.

He looked around the circle, and his eyes settled on his girlfriend.

"Laurel, truth or dare?"

"Dare."

"Pull down your pants and pull up your shirt and stay that way for ten seconds. I dare you."

Laurel stood up obediently. She lifted her shirt to her armpits and then pulled down her long johns and underwear to her knees. In the dark you could make out only her naked torso glowing in the firelight.

Cyrus began to count down.

"Ten . . . nine . . . eight."

I made brief eye contact with Isco, who averted his gaze under his fedora.

"Seven . . . six . . . five."

God, he was counting *excruciatingly* slow.

Viktor was rapt, smiling like a fiend at Laurel's nude body. The bottle of Jack was empty now, and crushed beer cans were starting to accumulate around his feet.

Gia and Noora both had painful smiles on their faces, but I wanted to jump out of my skin. I hated seeing a girl be so . . . submissive.

"FOUR THREE TWO ONE, she's done!" I yelled.

Laurel pulled her clothes back on and sat down.

An awkward tension hung in the air.

"God, just trying to have a little fun," Cyrus said.

Fun for who? I thought.

Truth or Dare was a big manipulation setup so he could scratch a pervy itch and trick us girls into titillating him, it was so obvious. I watched him as he scampered off to moon some unsuspecting campers at a nearby spot.

I had gone on this trip to get away from Dov, but his spirit was still there with us.

III

We crowded around the picnic table at midnight. Mushroom hour.

I had taken them only once before, when I drank a tea that tasted like dog breath in which the mushrooms had been steeping and then gone for a walk down Philly's South Street with friends. Everything seemed very large, very small, or very funny. I didn't have any glowing realizations, no life-changing revelations. But here, in the wilderness, I knew the shrooms would really shine, and I was desperate for some guidance.

Cyrus explained that we'd be eating them in pairs, because that's how it's done ceremonially. He laid out everyone's portion one by one on a scrap of paper towel on the table. When he got to me, he rummaged through the bag and pulled out two scrawny-looking ones.

I looked around at the other boys and their mushrooms. They were all chewing down way bigger ones than the ones Gia and I had been given. Were these backstock boys trying to hand themselves the opportunity to become more enlightened than us?

One giant, evil-looking mushroom remained on the table.

Isco suggested we cut it into a bunch of little pieces.

"No way, dude," Cyrus said. "Can't disgrace the sanctity of the sacred toadstool."

"Well, I think Cy should get it," Laurel piped in. "He brought them."

"Thanks, babe," Cyrus said.

The others were starting to filter back to the campfire, content with their dosage and ready to await the effects. But I stayed put—why should Cyrus the creep get the big shroom?

I tried reasoning with him.

"All the girls got tiny mushrooms, maybe we should split it so it's fair."

"Fair? *Ha.*" Cyrus snorted. "You girls get everything."

The enlightened shaman had disappeared.

"Cars, iPods," Cyrus said. "Dov pays *your* rent."

He looked right at me.

"No he doesn't," I stammered.

"That's not what I heard."

"I pay my own rent," I said louder.

"Kate isn't a Dov girl," Gia piped in.

"*Sure*," he replied.

I stared at the giant mushroom on the table while a wave of anger burbled inside me.

I worked the hardest out of anyone here. I took the shitty cities and made them flower—I hired half the people on this camping trip! Who did this little shit think he was? He should be thanking me, not insinuating I got where I did because I slept with Dov.

I snatched up the mushroom and shoved it in my mouth.

"There," I said, chewing. "Problem solved."

Cyrus went quiet as I swallowed it down. Enlightenment tasted disgusting—a mouthful of moldy pumpkin seeds. I suppressed a gag as I stomped back to the sanctity of my tent.

Just another reminder about how men were so entitled—always hogging more than their fair share—in the Big House, in business, in modeling, in mushrooms.

Twenty minutes later, when the world began to waver like a giant flowery dream around me, I began to have a tinge of regret.

Did I really need that giant shroom?

III

An hour later, Gia and I were sitting cross-legged when I began to notice that the tent had suddenly grown large as a cathedral around us. It struck me as very funny, and I laughed and laughed until my body couldn't *stop* laughing.

Gia had the giggles, too, but nothing like me. Involuntary peals of laughter were wracking my body like the side effect of something toxic, and they only stopped after I collapsed into a crumbled heap on the floor.

I rolled over and stuck my head out of the tent flap and saw the world had become one giant, moving pattern. I looked down at my arms and saw they had turned into waving filaments, too, in flux with everything around me. I was a wave of wheat in a giant cosmic field, and the only thing anchoring me to the here and now was my own silly little consciousness—something that the sacred toadstool had unrooted and tossed aside like a weed.

Doom started blurring my edges. What would happen if the universe simply absorbed me back up again? I zipped the tent flap back up and turned back to Gia. We would only be safe in here. It was our link to the physical world, the threshold of a door to perception I didn't want to fully open yet.

"I wanna go out. See the stars," Gia said, dreamily. Her hand made a move to unzip.

"Don't open it!"

"Why not?" she asked.

If she stepped outside that tent, that would be the end of her. She'd get swallowed up by the everything outside like a puddle on a hot day.

I tried to think of a reason without unsettling her.

"I hear like, lizards," I lied. "Jumpin' around out there."

Gia listened for a moment.

"I don't hear anything." She made a move to unzip the flap.

"Don't go!" I begged.

Gia turned to me, and in the moonlight I watched as her blond hair started turning black at the root. It raced down her back as wild as a vine, and before long it had grown so large and bushy it filled the entire tent.

Gia's face was reconfiguring into another, her features swimming together—her cheekbones became sharper, her eyes kinder. A different woman was in the tent with me now, wearing a white sheath and knee socks, looking pure and clean as a saint. My mom's hat—also white—sat on top of her head, the brim glowing like a halo.

Gia had completely disappeared, and Yoko Ono was looking back at me.

"Welcome," I cried, bowing low on the tent floor, where some stalactites had curiously sprouted up around me.

Yoko, sacred martyr! The blood of the Beatles projected onto her hands by a generation of racist pigmen. Why had she transported here all the way from the Dakota penthouse? She must have a very important message for me to come this far.

"Jeez," she said. "What is wrong with you?"

I gasped.

Of course Yoko knew.

"All these . . . men," I told her. "You understand," I said.

She nodded.

"Come on, you're coming with me," she said.

"No!" I screamed, digging my fingernails into the canvas floor of the tent. "If I go out there, I'll . . . dissolve!"

"Well, I can't leave you in here. Just come out where I can keep an eye on you." Her voice sounded tinny and high like Gia's.

I tried to get up and follow, but my legs folded underneath me and crept across the ground like knobby redwood roots.

Yoko picked up my root-legs, tucked them under her armpits, and skidded me out into the night on my belly. I lay facedown on a bed of pine needles, waiting to be absorbed by the terrible everything. Her footsteps reverberated into the earth as she headed toward the campfire.

"She's fine," Yoko said. "Just trippin' balls."

"Serves her right!" Cyrus yelled.

I rolled over to inspect the sky. It glimmered like a lake. I reached up to disturb its smooth surface. It began to reverberate, little concentric circles spreading out from where my fingertip touched down. I tapped the sky harder. A star shot from underneath my index finger.

I heard someone at the campfire say, "I totally saw that shooting star."

I smiled a secret smile to myself. See, I was still capable of making things happen for myself. Something was wrong—Yoko knew it, I knew it—but all the power to change it was somewhere in me. I could always make things happen for myself.

I melted into the ground, a perfect silver lake, and slid back into the tent.

III

I woke up a few hours later to the sounds of empty beer cans pelting the top of the tent. Gia was back to herself, snoring next to me on the air mattress. I poked my head out and saw Viktor up in the redwood, shirtless in the frigid night. He saw me looking and threw his head back and unleashed a howl into the night.

"*AWWOOOOOOOOOOO!!!!*"

Everyone else had gone to sleep, but Viktor was still wanting to party. In the time it took me to zip the flap back up again, Viktor had shimmied down the tree and was trying to force himself in.

"Lemme in," he said.

"Tent's full," I said.

Gia sat up next to me.

Just Viktor's head was poking into the tent like a huntsman's trophy.

"Lemme in, girls," he slurred.

"Get out!" Gia said.

Viktor had his shoulders in now, and he was using his sheer size to force himself into our tent. Gia and I pushed against him, but he wouldn't budge. He was so much stronger than us.

"LEMME IN," he shouted, pushing through harder. I could hear the aluminum poles start to bend, the nylon ripping.

He dove inside onto our air mattress as we escaped—I grabbed my keys and Gia's hand, and we ran toward the safety of my car.

The shrooms were still thrumming in my ears as I screeched out of the lot and down the road, leaving everything that was wrong with me behind us.

III

The sky was starting to lighten around the bridge.

It was a very famous bridge, the Bixby. The only way to get to Big Sur and back.

It cut a straight line across a chunk of coastal abyss that was still eerily black, even as sunset was dawning around it.

We pulled over on the side of the road to admire its glory.

As I stepped onto the Bixby, my skin was starting to prickle. I became acutely aware of every sensation pouring over my body—the air sharp as a knife against my nose, molecules of sea-foam salting the back of my tongue, the wind howling in my ears.

AWWOOOOOOOOOOO!!!!

My clothes—they were so tight, they were tugging at me. I could feel the scratch of every little label—AMERICAN APPAREL MADE IN THE USA. They were burning to come off my body *NOW*.

I started to run.

Halfway across the bridge I left my sweater in a heap on the road. Then I pulled off my Mélange Olive Thermal and pitched it over the side, feeding it to the sky. I yanked my U-neck Tank in Cranberry over my head, and it was soon floating like a ghost over the Pacific. Next was my Crossback Bra in Slate. I stretched it out and shot it over the bridge like a slingshot into the abyss. *Take that.*

No man's label could tie me down now.

I noticed Gia behind me was shedding her clothes, too. We were so close by then we could communicate telepathically.

Together we held hands and ran topless across the Bixby—the most photographed bridge in California—but there wasn't a single camera to be found. We did it just for us, a kind of baptism in the sun of the young day. A chance to liberate ourselves—to make things *right* when everything was going so wrong.

This was the concept we had been sold on—we were sexually autonomous women, the sole owners of our bodies and experiences and lives. That was what we'd thought we were accomplishing in the bathtub shoot, the shoots some of us did with Dov.

But now I could see the cosmic flaw in that plan.

There was still a man at the top manipulating all of us, exploiting us for his self-gain. He had built up his whole company to serve him like one big sexy Truth or Dare game, and we all had to play.

When I reached the other side of the bridge, I found myself there, naked and pure and only belonging to myself.

Now there was no going back.

13

The Change of Plans

That spring, I was able to take a rare week off. I had been with the company for a little over a year and hadn't taken a vacation. My mom used her time-share weeks for a place in Orlando, which her side of the family and their respective broods descended upon for spring break 2006. It was an impersonal, monolithic structure filled with swimming pools and orange trees and normal vacationing families.

I was really looking forward to it. Ready to do the good old-fashioned vacation thing—do the Sunday *Times* crossword with my dad, swap Aleister Crowley books with my brother. I was ready to spend some time with my *real* family. I had flown home for Christmas, but the chaos of the holiday was easy to absorb into, so I wanted the time to connect and become that version of myself I can only be with them—the baby of the family.

I was especially looking forward to seeing my sister, twelve years older than I am. When I was growing up, she was a teenage demigod upstairs in her bedroom, presiding over a domain of Lee press-on nails and Love's Baby Soft perfume. I idolized her—craving every second of her attention until the sad day she went off to college, and it was just me left at home. I remember watching her car drive down the hill until it disappeared into nothing, and a profound sense of loneliness filled me up that never really left. My brother, whose basement bedroom domain was one of tarot cards and Ramones records, had left for college one year earlier.

Sometimes because my siblings are so much older than I am, people ask if it's like being an only child. And while I never had to share my toys or wear someone else's sneakers (although I inherited all the 1970s hand-me-downs my practical mother stowed away, my first real vintage), that sacred specialness of being an *only child* was missing.

My parents had already seen it all. They'd been through all the milestones, twice—I couldn't simply glue macaroni to something and expect accolades. I had to go big to get attention, do more than my siblings had done before me. And by the time I was out of high school, I had accumulated an impressive list of achievements—class presidencies, writing awards, admission to Bryn Mawr—the most expensive accomplishment of them all.

It wasn't that I grew up poor—we leaned toward the upper end of middle class. My dad was a small-town lawyer in my hometown of Pringle (population 891), more Atticus Finch than Robert Kardashian, and my mom was a nurse who didn't work but kept up her registration just in case.

I got everything I ever needed or really wanted—guitar lessons, an American Girl doll for Christmas, kitschy clothes from the dELiA*s catalog. But when I graduated college, my mom exclaimed, "The gravy train is over!" and I knew it was time to pay them back by becoming totally self-sufficient and never asking for anything.

And so far I had been doing a good job. I was paying my own bills, and I had a blossoming career at one of the biggest fashion companies of the new millennium. That should have made them the proudest. But with the way I had been feeling about Dov lately, work was the last thing

I wanted to brag about. I had mentioned my "eccentric boss" a few times in passing—but my parents were total network news junkies. I could only keep the truth under wraps for so long.

I was planning on distracting them with my newest triumph—I was flying to Orlando from New Orleans, where I had just finished a particularly challenging round of scouting for the new store on Magazine Street. It hadn't even been a year since Katrina, and the city looked like a muddy parking lot from my window seat as the plane cleared the clouds and prepared to land in NOLA.

How would I find hipsters down there?

There was . . . *nothing*.

But the Factory was insistent—American Apparel needed to be there, as if to say that if our T-shirt shop could weather the storm, New Orleans would, too. I checked into a hotel on St. Charles Avenue, its lobby filled with flood mud and construction detritus and creepy candelabra light fixtures. It seemed like something out of a horror movie.

"Don't go out alone!" the bellhop warned me. I shared rides to the shop with rich tourists who were staying at the hotel for weddings, and other shows that must go on.

I stayed in New Orleans for two weeks—I ate my first raw oyster there—and when I was finally through scouting and hiring, that old sense of fulfillment was flickering again. American Apparel was making a difference in people's lives, conjuring opportunities like magic everywhere we went. That was the most important thing.

I'd just brag to my family about that, I thought, as I rolled my suitcase off the SuperShuttle and navigated the path to my family's time-share unit. I'd distract them with my triumphant story about manifesting jobs out of a metropolitan mud bog in New Orleans instead of my wanking boss on *20/20*.

When I saw my parents, I was surprised to see that they looked a little older than the last time I'd seen them. It made me realize just how far away California really was, how long I had been gone. My sister would be arriving later that night with her kids, and I couldn't wait to see her, eternally the six-year-old waiting for her to come back from college and pick up where we left off.

The afternoon got off to a rough start when my eighty-five-year-old grandma caught a glimpse of me striding to the pool in my American Apparel String Bikini in Lipstick Red, a skimpy nylon triangle top and barely there bottoms that tied on the sides. It channeled Phoebe Cates in 1982's *Fast Times at Ridgemont High*, the specific design inspiration cited by Roz at the Factory.

My grandmother didn't seem to get the reference.

"*Katie*," she tsk-tsked, shaking her head at me. "Aren't you *ashamed* to be wearing that?"

The statement nearly knocked me over.

Ashamed?

I looked around at the time-share guests. It was all kaftans and giant tankinis sagging off granny bottoms. Modesty ruffles, placed to disguise. Translucent T-shirts floating shapeless as jellyfish around people bobbing in the pool.

It wasn't exactly the string bikini crowd.

But *ashamed*? Did I feel ashamed?

Shame, over something as nonnegotiable as my body? After a year at American Apparel, it was something I had never even considered. By then I felt total ownership over my body—I was comfortable in my skin, wearing whatever I wanted whenever I wanted. These were the concepts that always kept me going—even in the chaos of a maze, a lab rat could find a little bit of sugar.

But should I have worn something more modest around my family? I hadn't even thought of that. A bikini in steamy Florida weather seemed like a natural choice.

I suddenly felt very naked and reached for a towel.

"Sorry, Gram," I began. But apologizing felt wrong, too.

My aunt Jane swooped in to the rescue, rolling her eyes.

"God," she said. "What is *wrong* with our family?"

I guess every family—natal or corporate or otherwise—has their own problems.

III

My sister arrived a few hours later.

One thing about my sister, Ellen, is that she suffers from a terminal case of middle child syndrome. In her quest to become special, she's gathered a doctorate and a private practice and two businesses and children who aren't even annoying, and she always has time for me and will drop anything when I call. Lately our sisterly relationship was shifting into something tighter, more secure. I was finally getting to know her as an adult, and I needed her advice.

I was still wearing my bikini of shame when we convened in the hot tub, along with my mom and Aunt Jane. This was always my favorite part of our vacations, hearing the family tabloid straight from the mouths of the matriarchs, who always had the best dirt.

But this time the women only wanted to talk about me. I engaged step one of my plan and prepared to stun them with my New Orleans story, but Ellen cut me off.

She had seen the *20/20* with Dov and John Stossel, two formidable mustaches dueling under the studio lights. Dov squirming, speaking in Clinton-ese, insisting he never slept with the plaintiffs of the sexual harassment lawsuits.

"I've never had any intimate intentions with these women."

Now I was the one squirming. I'd always artfully tucked Dov away when I talked about the company before. But now, the jig was up.

Everyone could see he was a perv, but they were missing all the other important details. Couldn't we just keep talking about the great job I'd done in New Orleans?

Ellen was a clinical psychologist and offered a hypothesis after watching the interview.

"Does he sleep much?" she asked.

I said I didn't really know about his sleeping habits.

"Thank God!" my mother yelled.

I wondered what that had to do with anything. But I suspected Dov didn't get much sleep, and come to think of it, I'd never seen him eat much either. There was always the promise of eating or acknowledgments of hunger, but I had never actually seen him consume anything other than Nescafé instant coffee.

My sister said she thought he might have the kind of personality type that a lot of successful CEOs had—it was almost like a superpower.

"Hyperthymic temperament," she said.

> Abnormally high levels of energy.
> Extreme extroversion and self-confidence.
> Chronic risk-taking.
> Lack of inhibitions.
> Increased libido.

It hit me like a lightning bolt.

Dov's grueling work ethic—the same one that he forced all of us to adopt—was actually a *disorder*. He wasn't a maverick—it was pathological.

Before I could stop myself, the story about Dov and Caralee in the dressing room spilled out. I watched my sister's mouth drop open, saw my aunt's shocked expression. My mom, looking worried.

It felt so good to see someone finally *shocked* by Dov's behavior. Relief started to pour over me. I hadn't realized how much I needed to share, how much I needed to talk about everything that had been going on, everything I had buried. To hear some advice from women I really could trust—my real family, who only had my best interests in mind.

"He said he was *trying something on*," I recounted.

My sister made a bitter face.

"Just keep your nose out of it and work," my mom advised, resorting to bootstrapping Boomer logic. "A job's a job."

But going along with everyone and not making waves is what had sunk me so deep into this misogynist hell pit already, hadn't it?

I looked to my sister for some psychological advice.

Wait until she got a load of Aika the geisha, the company-sponsored vibrators, the mysterious photo database at the Factory that I was beginning to suspect functioned as one big spank bank for Dov. I was getting ready to tell her everything—unleash a total trauma dump—when my father interrupted us, appearing by the hot tub with my Nextel in his hand.

"This thing's going crazy," he said.

I hopped out of the tub and snapped it open.

Thirteen missed calls from the Factory?

Why were they calling me *here*? I had cleared my vacation with Ivy months ago, and I made sure all the Hollywood stores were fed with employees before I left. There were no new stores on the pipeline this week. What could they possibly need from me while I was with my family?

I headed into the tiny bathroom in the unit where I could have some privacy. A garland of drying swimsuits hung from the shower rod overhead, and the smell of Coppertone was in the air—cruel reminders that I was supposed to be on vacation, enjoying myself.

The phone rang again as soon as I shut the door. It was Ivy.

"Listen, I know you're on vacation, but Dov needs you in Miami. It's a total disaster down there and—"

"What do you mean?" I cut her off.

A stony silence filled the line.

I'd never been short with Ivy before. But after the massacre of my hat and the Paris video she'd never bothered telling me about, she was surging to the top of my shit list.

"I got this vacation approved last month," I said.

"Well, you didn't get it . . . preapproved."

This time I went silent.

It was easy to decode the meaning—I hadn't asked Dov *personally* if I could take this vacation, and now he wanted to yank me out of it.

"Luckily you're already in Florida, so you can fly into Miami tomorrow first thing," Ivy continued. "He'll be waiting for you at the South Beach store."

The line went dead in my ear.

That was that. There was no use in arguing. I had to go.

I felt that loneliness creeping again—the kind I felt when my sister left, but this time I was the one heading out, leaving everyone behind.

I shuffled back to the hot tub to break the news.

"What?!" My mom was outraged. "But you just got here!"

I looked at Ellen to see how she would react. She tried a more psychological tactic.

"This just means that you are indispensable," she said. "You're so important to the company, they can't function without you. *You're indispensable.*"

When I went to sleep that night, I tried it on. Maybe she was right. Maybe whatever needed to be done in Miami was a job that only *I* could do. Why else would they tear me away from my vacation? I was a businesswoman, and this was just yet another sacrifice for the greater good. I wasn't just some pathetic underling, jumping into obedience because Dov demanded it.

I was indispensable.

I'd go with that to lessen the sting.

III

I had the first and only anxiety attack of my life that morning on the way to the airport.

When I woke up, it was still dark out, but my mom was up already, waiting for me in the tiny kitchen, stirring up a little bowl of instant oatmeal for me in her Vanity Fair department store robe. It was so comforting, like I was back in high school. I gave her one last hug and tears filled my eyes—who knew when I'd get the time off to see her again?

I was prepared for a chill ride as I settled into my SuperShuttle seat. Flight anxiety was genetic in my family, and my parents made sure I was off with plenty of time to make it to the airport. I should have been feeling completely at ease.

But something was wrong.

We had just pulled out onto the orange-grove-lined highways of Orlando—no traffic, a straight shot through the Florida flatlands to the airport—when a strange sensation overtook my body.

My arms and legs started tingling, and a million stinging pinpricks pulsed over my chest. I unzipped my nylon jogger as a wave of nausea pulsed through my belly. My head started swimming with heat, and I couldn't catch my breath.

What was wrong with me?

I dug out a bottle of water from my bag and took tiny sips as a torrent of watery saliva rose up to gag me.

I looked at myself in the driver's rearview.

My face was gray-green, but my neck was beet red.

When I identified what was happening to me as a panic attack, I still couldn't make sense of it. What did I have to be panicked about? I had made the shuttle, I'd make my flight.

Everything was fine.

I wanted to scream at myself—*Chill the fuck out!*

But my body was freaking out, it wouldn't listen to my brain. It couldn't hear it through the deafening ringing in my own ears. I laid my head on the cool window and concentrated on my breathing—a deep inhale through my nose, a long exhale through my mouth—and by the time I arrived at the United Airlines terminal, I was starting to feel OK again.

When I boarded the plane to Miami and sank into my plane seat, I was so exhausted I fell right asleep. But when my body had finally clocked out, my brain decided it was time to take over, and it lit up with a demented dream.

In it, I was moving into a giant, dilapidated company apartment full of American Apparel girls. We had every floor of the house—a creaky, rotten death trap in an area of town that hadn't even been gentrified yet. The house was just like the set of the Rolling Stones video—ready to be torn down—but Dov got a deal and crowded us all inside to save money.

I got assigned the shittiest room of all, the most unstable one in the house. If I walked too quickly into one corner, the whole floor groaned and shifted under my weight like a pinball deck. The moldering wood was threatening to collapse under me, crackling and splitting while I hopped around, searching for a stable spot.

This house is unsound! I want to scream.

But all the other girls either don't mind or don't notice. Their rooms aren't in as bad a shape as mine. And I don't want to be a complainer, so I don't say anything. I just tough it out and cross my fingers that the floor won't open completely and swallow me whole.

I just go on pretending that everything is fine.

"Welcome to Miami, home of the Dolphins, where the local time is nine thirty-four A.M.," a voice crackled from the cabin speakers.

I snapped out of the dream with a yelp.

An old lady next to me looked over with concern.

"It's a sizzling ninety degrees outside, we hope you have a pleasant stay in Miami or wherever your future destination may be," the pilot continued.

I took a deep breath and wiped the sweatslick from my forehead.

"Are you all right, dear?" the old lady asked.

I nodded, panting.

I was fine, now that I was awake. The dream was over. Or so I thought.

I went on to have that dream again and again.

The American Apparel House Dream, I call it.

I guess it's really a nightmare. I always wake up from it with my pj's damp and clinging to me, my heart pounding, my throat so dry I choke. And then the overwhelming sense of sweet relief takes over as I sink back into my clammy pillow—*Relax, it was all just a bad dream.*

I still have the dream to this very day. Whenever life gives me uncertainty or illness or sadness, my dreams light up like a stage, and the whole cast of American Apparel comes trotting out for an encore. They resurface when my conscious is unguarded and distracted by its current worry to sneakily pull me back to that other time in my life when I felt so helpless and out of control.

14

The Versace Mansion

It wasn't even 11:00 A.M. yet, and South Beach was already a patchwork of towels and partying spring breakers. The American Apparel store on Ocean Drive was directly across from the beach, a tropical paradise just steps from its front door. I couldn't resist a quick beach stroll to check out my new environment before I'd check in with Dov at the shop and see what the plan was.

Miami wasn't like any other city I'd been sent to before.

It was a top-tier, sexy city, throbbing with nightlife and adventure—a city on the top of any Dov girl's list. But this time, I was the one being rewarded. All my hard work and dedication was finally being acknowledged. I had officially made it to the top, which is what I wanted all along. I'd been hearing rumblings about a store opening in Australia but always assumed it would be a Dov girl going. Now I saw my chance to tie down something like that—everything would pay off, if I just held on.

The sunshine was dazzling as I rolled my suitcase off the sidewalk and tugged it toward the ocean, the hot sand squeaking under my heels. The sun beamed down on me and all my great accomplishments, when all of a sudden I saw something ahead of me that stopped me dead in my tracks.

A topless woman, stretched out in front of me, sunbathing on a striped towel.

It was like a good omen that I had made it to the right place.

Her eyes were closed and there was a smile on her face as she bobbed along to her headphones, oblivious and unbothered by the stares of volleyball-thwacking jocks in her midst. I looked around and saw another. And there, another! And next to her, there were two more. A pair of topless women, speaking Cubano, swapping a bottle of San Pellegrino back and forth.

What was this magical place I had discovered? Fearless, topless women were everywhere! They were unashamed in their nakedness, exuding the kind of can't-be-fucked-with-ness that no man would dare cross.

I smiled out at the paradise full of self-assured women around me, ready to take my spot among them. It was time to feel my power, whip my top off, and abolish my tan lines in front of the world, too. I was just starting to pull my T-shirt over my head when my Nextel chirped, snapping me back to reality.

It was Dov.

"Where are you?" he demanded.

"I'm at the beach, I just thought I'd—" It tumbled out of my mouth without thinking.

"The *beach*? What the hell are you doing there? I need you at the store."

Click.

The phone went silent, a dumb rock in my hand.

Shit, I thought. Already off to a bad start. Why did I tell him I was at the beach? I knew there was no mixing business and pleasure at American Apparel—unless you were Dov, of course.

I rolled my suitcase off the beach and back onto the sidewalk. The topless women—my fearless sisters—would have to wait a little longer for me.

III

"Swim and sex!" Dov yelled.

He pointed at me as I walked in the door.

"SWIM AND SEX!"

He yelled louder, as if I hadn't heard.

Hello to you, too, I thought.

"Latinas love mesh. They want to feel sexy," he continued, ranting. "I want all mesh and bodysuits in the windows stat. Maybe that's how we'll turn this sinking ship around."

A sinking ship? This was the first time I had ever heard an American Apparel store described that way. Hearing it from Dov's mouth made it seem even crazier. What was he talking about?

I looked around the shop. It appeared to be the perfect, glistening prototype of a successful American Apparel store. It was massive, stretching nearly a half block, and was stocked with all new styles hot off the assembly lines of the Factory. New girls I hired just a few weeks ago winked from the walls in brand-new ads. Fancy halogen lightbulbs dangled from industrial-looking fixtures overhead.

The only thing it was missing was customers. And where were all the other girls? The place was empty, just him and me.

"Come!" he barked, leading me over to a spot in front of the 2001s.

"See this square?" he said.

I looked at the floor tile he was pointing at, scrutinizing it for dust. It looked normal to me. Did he want me to clean?

"Do you know how much rent I pay for THIS TILE every day? Do you know how many T-shirts we have to sell daily to pay the rent on THIS TILE?"

I shrugged. Didn't he realize I was a scout?

"At least *three*. At least *three T-shirts* every day to afford this tile alone. Now look around," he commanded, gesturing at the floor.

I looked around.

"LOOK AT HOW MANY FUCKING TILES ARE IN THIS SHOP!" he roared. "I need you to get behind that cash wrap, and don't leave it until you tell me we're selling three T-shirts per tile in this shop."

I nodded obediently like a TV genie. *Your wish is my command, Master.*

Over the next few hours, I started to figure it out. Dov's insistence on signing a five-year lease on a new store a few blocks from Versace's mansion in the heart of South Beach was proving to be a shit sandwich of an investment. Ocean Drive was a party street full of bars and restaurants, not boutiques and retail shops. Tourists came in to drunkenly abuse the bathroom, not drop hundreds on ethically manufactured T-shirts. Bathing suit sales were middling, and with rent at a 3K a day, the store's traffic couldn't sustain the rent. Dov hated losing money and arguments, and South Beach's failure was driving him insane.

"MY DICK'S IN FLORIDA!" he'd scream into the phone at some underling back at the Factory. "AND IT'S NOT COMING BACK UNTIL WE'RE MAKING MONEY HERE!"

Click.

Dov had jumped into the action himself, assembling a team of allstar employees to descend upon the city, and I was the first to arrive.

Lucky me.

III

As I stationed myself behind the cash wrap, a sense of déjà vu settled in, like I was back at the Sunset store starting all over again. It dawned on me that *this* is what I'd be doing in Miami. I wasn't here to scout, to flit through the city and dole out jobs and sun my titties—I was here to try to pull off the impossible, to hunker down and save an unsalvageable store.

I wasn't here as a reward, I was here to pull off a Hail Mary.

As long as Dov's dick was in Florida, I would be, too. The duty of running the shop alone had been placed squarely on my shoulders and glued me there like flypaper. Dov had fired most of the employees the day before I arrived, blaming them for the bad sales. The only one who remained was Marisol, a teenage part-timer who wasn't a ton of help. I wondered how she had survived, but when she breezed in that first afternoon trailed by a curtain of long hair and still in her field hockey cleats, leaving little hexagons of dried turf trailing behind her, I knew immediately. She was Dov's type. He went uncharacteristically silent in her presence, and when her boyfriend stopped in later on her fifteen, he took me in the back room and exploded.

"That girl, she drives me crazy! She makes my heart beat so fast. *Feel*." He grabbed my hand and pressed it to the terry cloth there. "Outta my chest, right?"

Touching him like that, feeling the heat of his body, made me jerk my hand back. It felt so intimate. He kept ranting.

"Eighteen-year-old girl, eighteen-year-old brain. So stupid."

He wiggled his hand around his head and made the explosion noise that boys use with toy cars, colliding them together. "I could give her anything she wants. She doesn't care. She brings in that eighteen-year-old boyfriend. Are you kiddin' me!"

He pounded his fist on the folding table.

My mind reeled. I had never seen Dov jealous before—I thought that was antithetical to the concept of the brand. But here was Dov, raging with envy over Marisol's boyfriend, who still had braces on his teeth. It was truly pathetic.

In that moment, looking at Dov, red-faced and pacing around stacks of his own product like a trapped animal, I felt a flash of something for him that I hadn't ever felt before.

In the past year, I thought I had felt it all. At first, I had been cowed by his celebrity, eager to please him, driven by his mission. Then, lately, disgusted by his double standards, confused by his hypocrisy.

But now that I was watching an adult man, nearly forty, the powerful millionaire CEO of one of the biggest companies in the fashion world, obsess over a senior in high school, I started to feel something else.

Pity.

It was all so *pitiful.*

All his power and mythos instantly evaporated. The curtain had been pulled back, and despite all the fuss, there was just a child back there. Are all powerful men really just little boys, finally being able to attain with money and power what was never in their grasp? How had I never seen this before? It was so obvious to me now.

The only thing to do would be to fix up Miami as quick as possible, return home to LA, and then, when I could take a breath, figure out my next step.

I had to dig myself back out again.

III

Nyla told me there was no room for me at the girls' apartment in Miami.

I could tell by her tone that she was lying—of course there was enough room. Dov had instructed me to stay there for the duration of my Miami trip, and who knew how long that was going to be? But Nyla had never liked me, and I didn't like her either. When our paths crossed in Hollywood and I was assigned to scout for her store, she'd made it clear that she thought I was a turf invader and was so critical of my new hires that I learned to stay out of her way and just let her fill her store herself.

I knew the real reason why Nyla didn't like me.

It was hard to pin down, but it started to dawn on me in Miami, when she wouldn't share that apartment. Caralee and Junie and the other girls who slept with Dov liked me because I wasn't sleeping with him. I was no competition to them, just a girl on the sidelines.

But Nyla hated my guts *because* I wasn't sleeping with him.

She resented me for climbing the ranks without being a Dov girl myself, and she was going to make things as difficult for me in Miami as possible. She was stationed at the nearby Coconut Grove store, which wasn't in as much trouble as South Beach, and had claimed the apartment as her own.

I was left with two options.

I could call the Factory and beg for a hotel room in South Beach during spring break, when prices tripled, hemorrhaging more funds into the bottomless Miami money pit. That wouldn't work.

Or I could tattle to Dov about Nyla not letting me stay in the apartment, but that obviously wasn't a viable option, either. I'd rather sleep on a bench than complain to him about anything.

Fucking Nyla, making me scramble like this. She did this on purpose, to make me look weak and helpless after I had come so far and was finally on an even playing field with her. Australia wavered in the background, a prize for the most deserving American Apparel girl. I wasn't going to let her take it from me.

I whipped up a foolproof plan—I'd head to the boys' company apartment and take over a bed there. They'd make room for me. I was a big shot now, they had to listen.

III

The Versace mansion was creepy in the dark. On my walk to the boys' place, I stopped to gawk at the front gates, where Gianni Versace had been murdered almost ten years ago.

Right there, on *those* steps.

The mansion had an eerie presence reserved for crime scenes and battlefields, the air of tragedy swirling in the twilight. Here was a powerful man at the top of his game, going about the motions of his everyday life, thinking he was invulnerable when he wasn't. I remember seeing a photo of his black sandal, kicked off in the scuffle. It had a Versace logo stamped atop it, absurdly, resting in a pool of blood. A chill ran through me. Death and designer labels don't go.

Rihanna's new single "SOS" drifted from the radio of a taxi nearby, pulling me back to real life.

That first night when I was getting ready to leave the shop, Dov put me on salary.

He offered his hand for a shake. "Thirty thousand," he said.

I stuck my hand out automatically, and before I knew it, the deal was done. At first I let myself get excited—no more annoying weekly time cards to submit, a regular check coming every week no matter what—but then I realized overtime was a thing of the past. I had worked a twelve-hour day today and would be paid as if I had worked an eight. I was making the same amount as before, but I was giving him total ownership of all twenty-four hours of my day. Getting put on salary like the other Dov girls had always been the ultimate goal. Now even that was turning to shit.

How would I be able to get out of here? I belonged to him now, entirely. I wasn't sleeping with him, but what did that matter? I was still under him.

III

When I knocked on the door of the apartment, which was on the second floor of a crumbling complex a few blocks from the ocean, I didn't expect Viktor to swing the door open.

"Mama!" he yelled, pulling me in for a hug.

"What are you doing here?" I said, more sharply than I meant to.

But really, *Viktor*?

He was just a backstock boy. What could he do here that would be of any help? It was really taking the shine off my own invitation.

"What kind of hello is that?" he replied, going in for the hug anyway. "Dov asked me to come. He rented me a Vespa to zip between the stores, I'll give ya a ride."

He raised his eyebrows, and I knew what kind of ride he meant.

"No thanks," I said, pushing past him into a room filled with broken IKEA furniture. On the coffee table sat an abandoned bowl of mac and cheese with green fuzz creeping over it. A dozen empty beer bottles that doubled as ashtrays were strewn around the room. On the wall hung a few AA ads ripped from the back pages of *Vice* and hung haphazardly with packaging tape. The air smelled pungent, like a hamster's cage.

It was hell. Boy hell.

How low had I sunk here?

"Where's my room?" I demanded.

"I'll give you the master and sleep on the couch, mama. It's all yours."

Good, I thought. At least we had one thing straight around here.

I rolled my suitcase into my new room. It was bare, except for a mattress on the floor with a tangle of American Apparel terry cloth beach blankets on top, doubling as sheets. I noticed a set of double doors leading out to a tiny balcony. I stepped outside and was greeted by the blank expanse of the ocean. I looked up, hoping for stars, but there were none. A plume of jasmine crept up the trellis below, and the smell of it filled the salty air, reminding me I was somewhere tropical. Somewhere exotic. *Paradise.*

I'd been so excited when I arrived, but all that awaited me in Miami was grunt work for a pittance and a room in the stank boys' apartment. I started thinking of the topless women, how I'd never get a chance to set foot on that beach again. There would be no days off now. No *hours* off, even. And I gave up my family vacation for this.

It was all so terrible I had to laugh.

"What's so funny?" Viktor said. He could hear me from the living room, giggling like a freak.

"Nothing," I said, heading back inside.

"You wanna watch *Get Rich or Die Tryin'*? I burned a DVD before I flew out."

"Sure," I said.

What a metaphor.

"Put it on."

15

The New Arrival

A week later, a giant box arrived at the South Beach store, shipped overnight from the Factory. Inside was another batch of new art that Dov instructed me to change out yet again.

It seemed pointless.

In the past week, we hadn't sold more than a few hundred dollars' worth of terry towels and flip-flops each day. The floor tiles were not supporting themselves, and new art on the walls wasn't going to make any difference. This store was a stinker and Dov was in denial. All week he had been trolling the sidewalks of Ocean Drive late into the night, screaming into his phone and handing out 20-percent-off coupons to lure tourists in. Then he'd turn up again in the morning, wearing the same clothes, waiting at the door for me to open the shop for the day.

I slid my cutter along the edge of the box and wondered who the Dov girl of the week might be. I expected to see Junie's face. She was appearing in a ton of ads lately, despite all the havoc she had been causing back in LA. Right before I left for Florida, Caralee told me that Junie had driven her Mercedes up the stairs a *second* time. That explained why she was everywhere. Dov was giving her whatever she wanted, placating a spoiled child he couldn't control anymore. Just another example of the big sham—he wasn't nearly as strong as he wanted everyone to think.

What a . . . *pussy*, I thought. I caught myself smiling for the first time in days. It felt good, indulging in a little bit of thoughtcrime. I popped open the lid and peeled back the tissue paper.

My breath caught in my throat.

It was the last person I ever expected to see in an ad.

Dawn, the first girl I ever hired back in those early days at Sunset. I'd brought her into the company just about a year ago, when she was still a junior in high school.

Dov was thirty-seven.

I steadied myself on the corner of the cash wrap as the floor started to spin out from under me. I didn't want to look, but I couldn't stop myself. As I pulled each shot from the package, the story told itself.

My heart tanked when I recognized the location—the sweeping driveway, the giant steel door, the Silver Lake reservoir looming in the background.

Dawn was at the Big House.

In the first shot, she stood on the patio in a pair of silver disco pants, the sun in her eyes. In the next one, she's made it inside and is on her way upstairs.

Don't go up there, Dawn! I want to yell. But it's too late—she's crossing the threshold of the master bedroom now, looking back coyly, and I can't stop her.

Dawn was so young. What would have happened to me if I met Dov in high school? I was twenty-five now and still no match for him.

I had to see how the story ended, though I already knew how these things went. It was the big cliché of every horror movie—the girl's going to get it in the end.

In the next shot, Dawn's under that feather duvet that I recognize right away from all the other ads—Dov's duvet. A static white backdrop with only the girls changing out. I wondered how many nearly identical shots were cataloged in the database at the Factory.

There's two more shots in the stack, and I have to look.

Now Dawn's eyes were closed, her face contorted with ecstatic pleasure, or some teenage girl's approximation of it. I felt my throat start to tighten—like it always does when I'm in trouble, about to be caught.

In the very last one—the worst one—a hairy thumb pushes itself into the wide O of her mouth.

I knew whose thumb that was.

I dropped the stack of photos, and they spread across the floor like a smear. I crouched down to pick them up and fought the impulse to destroy them. Rip them into a million pieces and throw them in the alley dumpster, not hang them up for everyone to see.

Hot tears blurred my eyes. I couldn't see anything anymore.

I turned the blame inward. This was *my* fault. I had brought Dawn into the company and handed her right over to a predator. I was just as bad as Dov, using the girls as a stepping-stone to climb to the top, powered by my greedy ambition. I felt guilty—more guilty—because I was one of them, a trusted big sister shepherding them in, telling them all was well, ignoring all kinds of awful behavior that I *knew* was wrong.

Look around, for fuck's sake. The fluorescent lighting, the iPod pumping generic retail jams, the sexy girls on the walls.

This wasn't a revolution—it was just a *T-shirt company.*

I had scouted the girls like a cult devotee. I sized them up and took their pictures and handed them over for a paycheck and an empty promise.

Only a year had gone by since I'd joined the company.

How quickly I'd become a stranger to myself.

III

That night I hoped to arrive at an empty apartment. In the last week, I'd hardly seen Viktor around. During the day he zipped between stores on his Vespa, making his own schedule, taking time to light joints on the beach and chat up bikini babes. At night he'd hit up the South Beach bars, staying out until they closed at five in the morning. It was infuriating—I was chained to the store under Dov's watchful eye, and my hours off were so precious I needed to fill them with sleep, not partying. Tonight I was ready to have the place all to myself. I needed some quiet and space to figure out my next step.

As I walked up the stairs to the second-floor apartment, I thought about maybe calling Dawn. But when I rehearsed my end of the conversation, I came up with nothing. Would anything I said make a difference? She was a billboard girl now, intoxicated by all the power that comes with that. I'd seen it so many times by now. All the Dov girls operated under the illusion that they were the most important one—in a way, even I had, until just recently—and I would be powerless to convince her otherwise. She was in too deep now.

When I put my key in the lock, the door pushed open in my hand. Someone was in there. *Of course*, I thought. No quiet night tonight.

"Viktor?" I asked, peeking my head around the door. "Is that you?"

A tall, unshaven man in rumpled designer athleisure wear was smiling at me.

"Kaaaate!" he bellowed. He held out his arms like we were old friends at a high school reunion.

My heart sank.

It was Ian, the last person I'd ever want to see in that apartment.

Ian was brother to Roz, the art director of the company and alpha Dov devotee. Ever since that first day I saw her at the Factory, I'd regarded her with a mix of reverence and fear. Everyone did. She was the brainchild of the brand—the creative pulse of American Apparel that Dov could rest his fingers on. Roz had proven herself a cultural taste-maker, replacing the passé flannel-and-ripped-jeans uniform of the 1990s with the deep-V-and-disco-pants look of the new millennium.

She was a genius.

But her brother Ian was a total disaster.

"Figured you guys might need my help," he said, shrugging.

His *help*? I thought. I could have laughed, but nothing about this was funny.

Ian was a one-man wrecking ball with a salary and an expense account, rambling through the country on his own schedule. No one invited him to Miami, he simply booked a ticket and helped himself. He was an arsonist to productivity and a money waster—he rented expensive trucks and then forgot where he parked them, he got high and trashed company apartments like an entitled rock star. He'd show up to a store on an authoritarian tear, screaming orders at the girls, scaring everyone until a backstock boy would muscle him out and lock the door.

Any one of those incidents should have been enough to get him fired—he was a total liability. He needed rehab, not a company credit card. But getting canned wasn't in the cards for a nepotism hire like Ian. He was Roz's brother, and that was the only job qualification he needed.

Another thing that really bugged me was that Ian would never have passed the Polaroid test. All of us girls were held to the highest of physical standards, but Ian could roll in slovenly and unshowered in a stained T-shirt and Dov wouldn't say a word.

How different *American Apparel was*, I thought, looking at my new roommate, absentmindedly scratching his balls through his poly-silk basketball shorts. Nepotism and playing favorites was how every corporate business operated—there was nothing special about us there, either.

I washed my face and crawled in bed, grateful for the lock on my door, which would safeguard me from Ian for the rest of the night. But just as I was drifting off, I heard a quiet series of raps.

I opened the door a crack, and Ian's face peered in.

"So do you know where the cruiser is? I'm trying to track it down."

Oh my God! Ian was the last person alive who should ever be entrusted with the absolute power of the Crown Vic cruiser. I had left it in the New York lot last. I traced a line across a mental map as far as I could get.

"I think it's in Seattle," I lied.

Soon I heard the apartment door swing shut and his heavy boots on the stairs, on his way out to sample the South Beach nightlife.

I buried my head under my pillow and remembered a story Caralee had told me a few months ago about Ian. He and Dov had gotten into an argument, and Ian was so scary-high, he punched Dov in the face.

When Caralee told me about it, I was overjoyed. *Finally!* Even Roz couldn't save him now. I couldn't imagine ever disagreeing with Dov, let alone having an argument with him. Ian had to be toast.

But Caralee said, no, he was staying.

"That's how men settle things," Dov told her, shrugging it off.

Nothing made sense here anymore. It was like there were no rules, or maybe there were—but the only one who knew them was Dov.

I tried to go to sleep but I couldn't get comfortable. I tossed and turned, searching for the cool side of the pillow.

I thought of the time I heard Roz at the Factory, giving her version of The Hustle.

This is American Apparel, we can do anything we want.

Back then, it had made me feel so free, limitless opportunities all within my grasp.

But now I saw the threat in it, the hidden meaning.

This is American Apparel. We can get away with anything we want.

III

I don't know how it started because I was asleep. But suddenly I wasn't alone in my bed anymore, and there was something tight, wrapped around my waist.

Was I dreaming again? Another nightmare?

A boa constrictor had gotten me, was trying to swallow me whole. I could feel its wet mouth on my ear, getting a start. I tried to strain out of its grasp, but it circled around me tighter.

I opened my eyes slowly and the company apartment bedroom swam into view. I looked down and saw two hands, creeping up, slipping under my tank top.

I jolted awake then—this was no dream.

The hands pulled me tighter, weighing me down. I reached down to push them away but they were strong, I couldn't get out of them. They were moving all over my body, over my breasts, running any place they wanted.

I tried to get out from under them, but I was pinned to the bed. My heart started pounding in my ears.

"Shhh. It's just me," a voice whispered close. It smelled like Jack Daniel's and cigarettes.

A strange buzzing sensation rose up inside me. I opened my mouth and let out a scream.

"GET OFF ME!"

I twisted my body around to see.

It was Viktor—in a pair of company briefs, crouching on the mattress and gripping both of my forearms.

His eyes were vacant and tinged red around the rims.

"Fucking CHILL, what is wrong with you?"

He took hold of my shoulders and pinned me down again.

My eyes searched the room wildly, looking for an exit. I had locked the door last night—how had he gotten in? I saw the balcony doors were open—he must have scaled the trellis.

I twisted my arm out of his grasp and made a move toward the bedroom door. He jumped in front of it, blocking it with his body. There was no way around him.

"CALM THE FUCK DOWN!" he roared. "What's wrong with you?"

I just needed to get through that door. I couldn't put together what was happening or what had already happened to my sleeping body, but I would figure it out on the other side of that door.

"LEMME OUT LEMME OUT LEMME OUT," I screamed, my only defense. "GET AWAY FROM ME!"

Maybe if I was loud enough, someone could help me. I felt vulnerable and helpless. A little speck of nothing, an animal in a forgotten trap.

I heard banging on the other side of the door, and relief flooded me. Someone was *here*.

"Let her out, dude!" Ian yelled.

Viktor wouldn't budge from his spot in front of the door.

We were both staring at each other, breathing hard. Waiting to see what the other would do. It was a battle of control now, and I couldn't win. He was over six feet tall, so much bigger than I was.

"WHAT THE FUCK IS YOUR PROBLEM?" Viktor roared at me. "I DIDN'T EVEN DO ANYTHING!"

Ian was pounding on the door now, I could see it shaking in its frame. Viktor got distracted for a second—he took his focus off me and turned to look. This was my only chance—I had to think quick. I balled my hand into a fist and slammed it into his crotch. It wasn't even that hard of a hit, but it was enough. Viktor folded in half, and I grabbed for the doorknob.

I ran down the stairs and out into the blackness, leaving everything behind me.

When I got out to the sidewalk, I could hear Viktor howling inside the apartment, raging into the night. Ian tailed behind me, trying to catch up. I heard the faint hum of the waves crashing on the beach, just a few blocks away. As the adrenaline subsided, I started to think clearly.

What had just happened up there?

Viktor in my bed, his hands all over me. As if our distant sexual history provided him with an entitlement to my body, and he just went ahead and helped himself.

A blinding wave of anger slammed into me, carrying me away.

What a fucking *creep*.

He shouldn't be working here—definitely shouldn't be traveling with the girls. I thought about the camping trip, him drunkenly crashing into our tent. He wasn't a safe person to be around—and neither was Ian. Why had I decided to *sleep* in an apartment with the two of them? It was a red flag anyone else would have spotted a mile away. I had become so blinded by trying to make things easy for the company, I had forgotten the very basics of protecting myself.

Ian and I piled into the backseat of a taxi, on our way to find a hotel.

"Did you see how I scared him off?" he said. "He was fucking SHAKING."

I stared at Ian. He was amped up, high off the chaos.

"It's a good thing I was there, huh?" he said.

All my anger started turning inward again—it was the only way to control it.

"Fuck!" I screamed, punching the back of the seat. I covered my face—I felt so ashamed.

It was only when the old cabbie turned back to look at me with concerned eyes and asked, "Are you OK, honey?" that I started to cry.

16

The Offer

"I'm going to give you the advice I'd give my sister."

That was how he started it.

A few months ago, that would have done it for me—here was the proof, right from the man himself, that I was different from the other girls. Special. More valuable. But now I could see the greasy fingerprints of manipulation all over it.

What kind of *family* would operate like this?

III

Dov was waiting for me at the store the next morning. I rolled in bleary-eyed, wearing the same cami and hot shorts I'd worn when I ran into the night. I was a jangle of nerves after spending a sleepless night sharing a hotel room with Ian at the South Beach Ramada.

I was too numb to argue when the desk clerk told us there were no vacancies—it was still the thick of spring break. But after she noticed my tear-stained face and bare feet, she took pity on me and gave us the only remaining one—two double beds and a broken shower. Ian paid for it with the company card. I listened to the hum of the AC and monitored his snores until the window transformed the room with the safety of dawn.

I was exhausted in every way possible.

Nyla—the traitor—was in my spot at the cash wrap, counting the register for the day. She wouldn't meet my eyes. She must have heard about what happened already.

Fuck.

First a wave of embarrassment rolled through me, and then a flash of anger—this was all *her* fault. I charged toward her, but Dov caught me by the elbow.

"Come on," he said. "We're going for a walk."

He pulled me out the door and down Ocean Drive. I followed behind, an object carried in his wake.

Word had traveled fast about what happened the night before. Ian must have told Dov, which meant he'd tell Roz, and then Roz would tell everyone at the Factory. I thought about the rumors traveling at the speed of sound all the way from Miami to LA, the narrative changing, slipping out of my control, becoming more sensationalized as it gathered strength like a tropical storm.

I felt all my powers leaking away, everything I had worked for. I had done everything *the right way* and still had somehow ended here— underneath a dogpile of awful men.

Dov looked behind his shoulder to make sure I was keeping up.

"I heard a guy got crazy on you last night," he said.

"I'm fine," I said, automatically. I *was* fine, wasn't I? I didn't want him—or anyone—to think I wasn't strong, that I couldn't handle this.

He nodded. I realized he hadn't even asked.

"Well HR is going to want to talk to you about this, they're going to make it a big thing. So let me give you some advice—the advice I'd give my sister."

He stopped walking and turned to look at me. It was the only time I had ever seen him stand still.

"Now I can't give you the advice I'd give a girlfriend, because you and I never got *jiggy with it*. So I can only give you sisterly advice."

My eyes wandered to the dumpsters behind him as I tried to make sense of it. How would the advice he'd give to a girlfriend be any different if she awoke to find someone groping her in the middle of the night?

He put a hand on my shoulder and looked into my eyes.

"We've got three hours before LA wakes up—plenty of time to get on top of this. So when HR calls, you'll be ready to tell them to fuck right off. You tell them you can handle this yourself—don't give in to *victim culture*."

He spat the words out like they were bitter.

"You're better than that, you're stronger. You need to act like a man about this."

This wouldn't have happened to a man, a voice in my head said. It ran through like a little whisper, but it was there. I was relieved to hear it again, that Bryn Mawr voice that I had been burying all this time. It always told me the truth.

A girl crossed our path then, on her way to the beach, a towel over her shoulder and headphones in her ears.

He broke my gaze and held out a coupon.

"Twenty percent off, just for you."

She took it and went on her way. I wished I was going with her, that Dov was just a weird stranger in aviator shades handing me a coupon on the street that I could crumple and toss into the nearest trash can when I turned the corner.

He stared at her as she walked away, a vacant smile on his face, the fog of sexual reverie clouding his eyes.

Then he snapped his attention back to me.

"Listen to me. Listen to this."

His voice was getting louder now, more insistent. "I want you to go out today and get an apartment, any apartment you want. You pick it out, I sign the lease. How about that? Your car still in LA?"

I nodded.

"Pick out any car here, I'll get it for you. You want a Mercedes? I like Cadillac, but I bet you like Mercedes. It's yours. All you need to do is this one little thing. Email them. Email them and tell them you got this."

Here was the offer.

Free rent, a company car. I could step into the life of a Caralee or a Junie, expensing every bit of it and saving my entire 30K salary for whatever I wanted. And I wouldn't even have to get jiggy with the king. Wasn't this everything I had wanted?

But this offer didn't feel like a reward for my hard work, a milestone I had reached because I had earned it.

It felt like a bribe.

Of course Dov didn't want HR to know what had happened with Viktor. He wanted to snuff out any potential scandal before it got a chance to spark, protecting American Apparel at any cost. The mounting lawsuits had driven him into protection mode—anything to save his company, to save himself.

I started searching for excuses, any reason I couldn't stay here in Miami and do what he wanted, but I couldn't come up with anything. My life outside of work had been whittled down to nothing a long time ago. The company had eaten everything up. No boyfriend, no friends who weren't on the payroll. Their allegiance was to Dov, not me. I had spent so much time traveling that I was untethered from Los Angeles.

American Apparel was my life now—I had nothing else.

"I have a cat," I said, thinly.

"Fuck your cat. You can have all of Miami, if you want it. Your own little thing going down here. You're bigger than LA, you could do so much more for me. How about you fix Miami, then I'll send you to Australia. You like that? Lotsa girls want Australia. Australia is yours. But first you have to write the letter. *Come on*."

"But what about Viktor?" I asked. "He shouldn't be working here anymore."

"That little prick will be *saluting* you after I'm done with him. Be an example to the other girls. Show them how to be strong."

All I wanted this whole time was to be strong, but this didn't feel like the way to do it.

I stayed quiet. He got louder.

"Come *on*. You know my ass is in a sling here."

He was getting more frantic now. More desperate. He tried another tactic, pulling out all the stops. I knew it was coming. I could spot the ramp-up a mile away.

He tried to pitch me The Hustle.

I couldn't believe he had the nerve to try it on me now. Didn't he know I knew it by heart? I had heard The Hustle a million times, in backstock rooms, in boardrooms, on the Factory floor, at the dinner table in the Big House. I had delivered it myself in every new city I scouted. Did he think I could be that easily swayed, a warm little lump of clay in his hand?

The 48 Laws of Power, *had I read it? Victim culture was for weak women, was I weak? Don't fall for conservatism cloaked as liberalism. This is the revolution!*

The Hustle was reserved for people who needed convincing, people who had something he needed. It always benefited him in the end. I recognized it even this way, turned all the way around with the blade facing me.

So phony, the voice in my head hissed.

My eyes slid down to his shoes. Sensible docksiders.

The same ones your dad wears.

Now I was really starting to see things how they were. I thought of how far I had fallen, how blind I had been. How sad and pathetic I was for even considering this offer. But deep down, I did want to write the letter. If something as simple as an email would make the events of last night undo themselves and disappear as if they had never happened, it would be the easiest way out. I didn't want anyone to know. Dov and I were on the same page about that.

Miami glittered all around me, a white-hot jewel of a reward. A realm of my own, an escape hatch in paradise. Australia—the ultimate prize—beckoned to me.

A balmy breeze swept in off the ocean and enveloped me.

"So are you going to do it?" he asked again.

I sighed.

He could wear you down to nothing.

17

The Emperors Club

Dov said I could take the rest of the day off, a rare kindness that I almost appreciated until I realized it was just another piece of the bribe.

"Get some sleep, and when you wake up, write the letter," he said. Then I could meet him back at the store to do some apartment hunting for my new place in South Beach.

I went back to the hotel and fell into a dreamless sleep. When I woke up the next morning, I checked out of my hotel room. The store was just a few blocks away, but I stuck my arm in the air and hailed a cab.

"Where to, miss?" the cabbie asked.

A faded grove of pine-scented Little Tree air fresheners hung from his rearview mirror. I put my duffel bag on the seat next to me and lowered my sunglasses.

"Miami airport," I said.

That morning I had used my first salary paycheck to buy a one-way ticket back to Los Angeles. By the time the cab was pulling into departures, my phone was starting to light up.

I ignored it.

I imagined Dov waiting for me at the store to let him in for the day, his panicked calls to Nyla when I couldn't be reached. Ordering her to rush over and fill in for me yet again.

I reached down and powered off my phone, tucking it back into my bag. My hands were shaking. Leaving Miami without doing what he demanded was the ultimate act of insubordination, and I knew I'd be punished. But instead of feeling scared and hopeless and out of control, turning off that phone made me feel stronger than ever.

It felt great to truly rebel, for once.

III

Squeaky Fromme was waiting for me back at my attic apartment in LA. She was hungry for love after a month of the scant affections of my pet-sitting neighbor, and I was desperate for some, too. I sank into my bed and buried my face in her fur. I read somewhere that cats' purrs have healing vibrations, lowering stress hormones while raising endorphins. I needed both.

I closed my eyes and relaxed—I was home.

I was sure my job had to be over—it was only a matter of time before I got a call from the Factory, asking why I was MIA. Did I quit when I left Miami? I wasn't sure. Would Dov consider that quitting? Or would he *fire* me? He valued loyalty above all other qualities, and I had disobeyed.

I looked around at my apartment—my $750 safe haven—and it started sinking in that I wasn't going to be able to afford this place much longer without a job. I could stick it out for another couple months while I job searched, but then what? Finding a new gig takes time, no matter how impressive I was sure my credentials were after more than a year at the company.

American Apparel Hiring Manager—I was sure everyone would jump on me right away.

Then I started thinking about my Honda outside—the $250

monthly car payments, the $150 insurance. *Shit!* What was life going to be like without those regular salary payments that were going to make things so much easier for me?

I realized I needed to buy some time.

I started thinking like a businesswoman again. I only needed a small financial life raft—a few more weeks at American Apparel—that I could cling to while I applied to and interviewed for other jobs. It was just another sacrifice I was going to have to make—but one that would benefit *me* in the end, this time.

If I just held my nose and smoothed things over with Dov, I could get a few more weeks out of him. He was a dirtbag, but he was paying my bills, and if a loyal servant like Ian could *punch* him and keep his job, maybe the desertion of my duties in Miami wouldn't spell the immediate end for me if I acted like I was loyal, too.

And if I was honest with myself—and it was getting easier to see the truth, now that my LA life was on the line—it was something I had really wanted to do deep down, even if I knew it was wrong.

I opened my laptop, and I wrote HR the letter.

I used words like *misunderstanding* and *blown out of proportion*. I said things with Viktor hadn't been *a big deal*, that they must have heard some crazy story through a cross-country game of telephone. I said I was sorry to leave Miami, but I needed time to think. I said I hoped Dov would understand.

As I pressed SEND, I felt like a traitor to myself—I obviously knew this was not the way to be strong—but what I wanted most was for the whole humiliating scandal to disappear. I wanted to pretend it never happened, to go back to how things were before while I regrouped. I'd be out of the company soon enough. I'd gather my paychecks and my self-esteem, and in a month or two, I'd depart on good terms with a decent job reference for whichever fashion company was lucky enough to snatch me up next.

A few minutes later a reply from HR came through, offering a phone call to chat about the events, if I ever wanted. I deleted it immediately. I wanted no reminders of Miami in my inbox—that vulnerable girl was *not* me.

A few hours after that, an email from Ivy arrived, asking me to head to Silver Spring, Maryland, the following week to scout and reminding me that the new shop on Huntington Beach needed an open call before I left.

My plan had worked—I could go on at American Apparel. And Viktor? He got to keep his job, too. There would be no repercussions for him, either. I ran into my assaulter a few weeks later, calmly folding 2001s in the backstock of the Los Feliz store.

Writing that letter did exactly what I wanted—it was as if nothing had happened.

III

Skipping around those hiring sites—Mediabistro and Monster.com and even Craigslist—was really starting to shine a light on how undervalued and underpaid I had been at American Apparel. Seeing all those listings filled me with hope—envisioning my new professional life working for a nice, *normal* company like Diane von Furstenberg—60K!—or Betsey Johnson—70K!—or hell, even the Gap, the crown jewel at 80K to 100K. I applied to them all, imagining the boring workplaces full of rules and regulations and promotions handed out because you earned them, not because you were shtupping your boss. It was worth wearing biz-cas for.

After I applied to the heavy hitters, I started submitting my résumé more indiscriminately. LA was home to countless nameless fashion upstarts that would be grateful for my expertise, I was sure. No matter how I was feeling about it, American Apparel was still a big deal in the fashion world, and who wouldn't want the woman responsible for a part of its great success?

I must have sent out fifteen résumés in that first afternoon, then I sat back and waited for the corporate world to come fetch their prize. First I heard from DVF, who told me to come back when I had more experience—six months as a hiring manager was still a bit green for them, they said. At first, the recruiter at Betsey Johnson seemed interested.

"Wow, over a year at American Apparel," she said.

"I learned a lot," I said.

"I *bet*." She laughed. "What's up with that owner guy? Is he *really* a creep?"

By the end of the conversation, it became clear that she wanted to talk about only salacious Dov dirt instead of what I had been doing to make the company succeed. I was a curiosity to her, a sideshow in the fashion business. The whole world saw me as a Dov girl.

The Gap didn't even bother emailing back.

All of the energy started draining out of my job search. It seemed like the only one impressed with all the work I had been doing at American Apparel was me.

III

I was dropping off the Huntington Polaroids at the Factory a couple weeks later when I heard the adoring horde buzzing through the hallway. I froze.

It was Dov at the center, his dick finally returned from Florida.

I looked for a door to duck into, a shadowy corner, but there was nowhere. His eyes found me in the crowd immediately, two dark lasers pinning me under his gaze. I braced myself.

"I knew you'd leave Miami," he sneered, breezing past me.

I watched him blast through the double doors onto the Factory floor—his rightful kingdom.

I knew what he really meant—*I knew you were weak.* And I couldn't argue with him—I *was* weak. I had tried to do the right thing and folded halfway through.

I went to sleep in my apartment that night feeling shitty, but the very next morning, I had a bite on one of my job applications. I leaped out of bed like someone awakening from a coma on a soap opera—full of manic joie de vivre and delirious hope.

It was a headhunting gig for a large entertainment company—I couldn't get much information from the email they sent—and they requested an interview for the very next day.

The time had come.

I was getting out of here!

III

The interview was in a small but fancy boutique hotel, situated inconspicuously on one of those steep streets that slalom down from the Sunset Strip. I was wearing a black American Apparel pencil skirt, which seemed official enough for a real job interview, and a pair of heels that pitched me forward on the sharp incline. I had to shuffle down the sidewalk to keep from tumbling head over heels.

The woman on the phone had been vague about the job. I wasn't sure exactly what the company was even called, but the Craigslist ad mentioned tremendous opportunity for growth and exciting travel opportunities, and it all sounded very glamorous. At the bottom, I saw the words that mattered most.

COMPETITIVE SALARY FOR EXPERIENCED APPLICANTS.

The hotel wasn't like anyplace I had stayed in with American Apparel. Giant bouquets of fresh flowers filled the tables, and my heels went off like gunfire as I walked across a gleaming marble floor. This was definitely a giant step up from the depressing Holiday Inn lobbies where I'd hold my interviews. The hotel guests were just as impressive—impeccably dressed businessmen of every age swarmed around me. I detected expensive suits by the sheen of their virgin wool. They wore gold cuff links and silk pocket squares.

I had never seen so many rich men in one place before, and they were all smiling at me. There was something strange about the *way* they were smiling at me. I couldn't put my finger on it, exactly, but it was making me vaguely uncomfortable. As I glanced at the reception desk, I noticed even the bell-hop was staring at me, smiling with all his teeth.

Why did it seem like *everyone* in the lobby had been waiting for me to get here?

All the hairs started to stand up on the back of my neck, and my pulse began to quicken. It was like my body was trying to tell me that something wasn't right here. Like it knew something my brain didn't.

I swept my eyes around the lobby and spotted a young woman at a table with a manila folder sitting in front of her. She had to be the one—she stuck out in the swanky lobby, in her normy infinity scarf and department store jeans, an oddity among the sea of posh businessmen. She was wearing no makeup, her eyebrows plucked down to nothing, and her hair was an unstyled disaster tied back in a tragic scrunchie. But there was something kind of comforting about this girl's total oblivious-ness to the state of her appearance, especially after I had been obsessing over mine and everyone else's for the past year.

This girl was like me when I first started. A nerdy college girl. The *old* me.

The *real* me, I corrected.

I forgot about the creepy men of the lobby and held out my hand.

"I'm Kate." I said.

"I'm Kate, too," she replied.

Perfect!

It was like I had gone full circle and returned to the beginning to meet myself again, like something out of *The Secret*. We were laughing over the coincidence when a man I hadn't noticed stepped out from behind her. He was much older than we were—at least in his sixties—with silver hair and wire-rim glasses. He wore a blazer over a turtleneck and a signet pinkie ring, which gave him a vaguely European air. I couldn't quite place his accent.

"So pleased to meet you," he said with a stiff formality, holding out his hand.

When I shook it, he pulled me in so close I could smell his Drakkar Noir. He lowered his voice until it was nearly a whisper.

"You know, our company's success relies on its confidentiality, and I'd hate to meet in a place where anyone could hear our . . ."

He jerked his head in the direction of the busy lobby.

". . . our *trade secrets*."

I nodded. Business was important stuff, I understood that by now.

The man smiled back at me.

"Would you mind popping up to the room, and we could talk more there?"

I looked at the bank of elevators in front of us. He made a move to press the button.

"No thanks," I said, quickly.

Something about going into a hotel room with a strange man in a turtleneck was making alarm bells ring out in my head.

"Can we just stay down here?" I asked politely. I didn't want to offend my potential future employer, but I couldn't understand what was so confidential that couldn't be talked about in a quiet corner of the lobby.

"Very well," he said, holding his palms up.

He led me over to a secluded table in the back of the lobby, the other Kate trailing behind.

"First things first," he said, clapping his hands together. "You have a very impressive résumé. We see you have a degree."

Finally!

It was the first time I'd dusted off my degree since I left Urban—and this man knew its real value. One step closer to having this top secret job in the bag.

"Our company is growing so rapidly, and I think a smart girl like you could do very well with us."

Kate handed him the manila folder. He pulled out a few photo-copied sheets of paper and spread them on the table in front of me.

The first one contained a list—

POLITICS

BUSINESS

SPORTS

ENTERTAINMENT

MUSIC

FINE ART

FASHION

REAL ESTATE

I ran my eyes down it. I didn't see a corporate logo anywhere—not even a name.

"What's the company called?" I asked. It seemed like a reasonable question, but the man artfully avoided it.

"Well, we serve many fields. And our fine reputation hinges on our ability to provide exactly what our clientele needs, but *discreetly*."

He ran his finger down the list on the paper.

"You'll be able to meet all kinds of influential people with us, and in a way, that is a kind of compensation in itself."

"Who are your clients?" I asked. Another reasonable question.

The man ignored me and flipped to the next piece of paper in the folder. He turned it around to face me.

It was a map of the world, sliced into time zones, major cities circled in red.

NEW YORK

LONDON

PARIS

ROME

TEL AVIV

"As you can see, there are also tremendous travel opportunities. The whole world is completely at the disposal of the right sort of applicant."

This man was talking in code, carefully circumventing my questions.

"I know that you applied to be a headhunter, but now that you are here, I wonder if you might be interested in being a *spokesmodel*."

An image of Ivy back at Little Joy flashed into my head.

"What exactly does a spokesmodel do?" I asked, just like I had asked Ivy.

He shuffled to the next piece of paper and held it upright, so I couldn't read it.

"To be a spokesmodel is far more lucrative than our headhunting position, and you would be a wonderful candidate, with your degree, your job experience. I can tell you're a very bright and interesting girl that would certainly resonate with our client base. Perhaps this can shed some light."

He put the piece of paper down on the table.

I saw a scale at the top, marked with dollar amounts that matched up a row of cartoon diamonds.

"We see you more on this end," he said, pointing.

FOUR DIAMONDS   *$1,500 per hour / $15,000 day rate*
FIVE DIAMONDS   *$2,100 per hour / $21,000 day rate*
SIX DIAMONDS   *$3,100 per hour/ $32,000 day rate*

I suddenly understood everything—this was a high-end escort service, looking for new girls to entertain a web of rich and powerful men across the globe.

My hands flew to my face, and I skidded my chair back from the table. My body, which had been on high alert this whole time, finally knocked itself out of the composure it had been desperately trying to maintain since I walked into this sketchy lobby.

I looked up from the table, and Kate's eyes met mine.

She had an amused smile on her face.

I could feel my skin start to tingle with embarrassment. How did I not *realize*? How did I end up here?

"This is . . ." I stammered. "This is *not what I thought it was.*"

Kate's smile grew hard.

"Well, what did you *think* it was?" she said.

I felt like the stupidest idiot alive.

"I'm sorry for wasting your time," I said and ran out the door, my heels pounding on the marble, my heart pounding in my throat.

The men were still smiling at me on my way out. It seemed like everyone in that lobby knew the reason I was there except for me. Somehow I had managed to get tricked *again*. And this time, it was almost literally.

I ran to my car and locked myself inside, vacillating between embarrassment and sheer terror. Would they follow me? Would they kidnap me, now that I knew their secret? Would I be knocked over the head and sold into sex trafficking?

My parents would be *so disappointed* in me.

I watched the lobby door from the safety of my Honda long enough to realize that no one was coming for me, and I screeched out of there. When I got home, I reread the emails and found a little blue hyperlink at the bottom of Kate's email.

www.TheEmperorsClub.com

It had been there all along. I just had been too blinded by my amazing new opportunity to see it. The whole thing was so mortifying—how naive could I really be? And I was getting used to the feeling—every time I tried to raise myself up and grab at the gold ring, I got smashed back down again, the boot print of the patriarchy stamped on my forehead.

The world really was just one giant Emperors Club.

On the way home, I started thinking how my job at American Apparel really wasn't *that* bad, in the grand scheme of things. Maybe I had been too hard on myself, on Dov. Things could be way, way worse. I told myself to be happy for what I had. I remembered what my mom had said.

Just keep your nose out of it and work. A job's a job.

Was I being too much of a hard-ass idealist, here? Hadn't that burned me enough already? And where else was I going to go? No one wanted me—the company had a bad corporate reputation, and I was guilty by association. On top of that, everyone I knew worked for the company. Was I going to leave all my friends and start all over? My life *was* the company—it sustained me in all kinds of different ways. I couldn't give all that up so fast.

I delayed my job search and kept on working at American Apparel. I told myself it would be just another three months, which quickly streamed into six. Then another year went by, and then another.

I never attempted to leave again.

Epilogue

L ike every cult, American Apparel met a tragic end.

Dov was ousted by a board of investors in 2014, amid more sexual harassment lawsuits. Without its creator at the helm, the company became unmoored and unfocused and found itself in bankruptcy court in 2015 and again a year later. In 2017, major wholesale T-shirt producer Gildan Activewear stepped in to pick up the pieces. They bought the brand name and then ironically moved production overseas. The Factory was shuttered not long after, and retail stores closed worldwide.

It was as if those outside forces Dov was always warning us about had finally descended and taken down everything we'd built. I watched it all happen from a distance, vacillating between satisfaction and dejection. It felt good to see him held accountable, but I couldn't help but feel crushed, seeing our utopia falling. There had been so much promise, but Dov had ruined it for all of us.

My end came much sooner than his. Over the course of my last two years with the company, big changes started happening at the Factory. American Apparel went public, so now it wasn't just Dov running the show but also a boardroom full of men in suits, who had to be contended with. Their influence resonated throughout the company and diluted Dov's authority, transforming American Apparel into a company as uptight and corporate as the Gap. That was the beginning of the end. Stores started opening in malls, and I watched from the sidelines as the girls in the ads got thinner and whiter. More commercial, more airbrushed. Boring.

It's just like Hollywood to take the thing that makes someone special—what made them stand out from the pack in the first place to *become* famous—and then run it through the meat grinder and pump out the same old hamburger for mass consumption. The same thing was happening to American Apparel.

In this sanitized version of the company, it was easier for me to avoid Dov. I still scouted for LA and the cities no one wanted—Salt Lake City was the last of my assignments—but the golden days were over. The company's growth was starting to plateau, fewer stores were opening, and I wasn't traveling nearly as much. When I did fly out, I was just going through the motions. I couldn't deliver The Hustle anymore—I saw Dawn in every new recruit's face.

But still, I stayed.

I floated along, paycheck to paycheck, anesthetized by the pleasures of Los Angeles—late-night drives to Ojai hot springs with the girls, Steve Aoki DJ nights, the thrill of eavesdropping on Lindsay Lohan and Samantha Ronson one table over at the Roosevelt Hotel. I wasn't totally sure of what I was doing or where I was headed or even if I was having a good time. But each Monday morning, I checked The Cobrasnake to see if I had made it into any of the weekend party pics, and when I'd see my face smiling back out at me, I always looked happy. A portrait of a girl having the time of her life in Hollywood.

But behind the scenes, turmoil was brewing. An ICE audit of the Factory in the fall of 2007 targeted the workers—most of whom were undocumented immigrant women—and the production slowed while a recession loomed ominously on the brink of 2008. The company—which had pulled in $260 million just the year before—started losing money fast.

That's when the first round of layoffs happened. They began at the bottom, as layoffs usually do, with the retail division. I was so numb at that point, I never saw them coming.

One sunny morning in April 2008 I was summoned to the Factory, and Ivy—the same person who brought me in—was now telling me I was out.

I was so shocked, tears slipped down my face before I could stop them. After everything I had given up, it was the ultimate betrayal. I was getting *kicked out*, stripped of my phone number and Nextel and my computer over something as impersonal as the company's bottom line.

I saw myself falling back into that dark hole that was always threatening to drop me straight back into Philly. I was asking myself the same stressful questions—a broken record of my own making.

How was I going to afford rent on my precious apartment?

Where would I work now?

How much longer could I really last in Los Angeles?

I was right back to square one.

A few days later, an acquaintance reached out with a sure thing—a job at CBS, working for the reality television show *Big Brother*. It paid $850 a week, two hundred more than my American Apparel salaried weekly rate. My ears perked right up.

"What's the job?" I asked.

"Typing and taking notes," he said. "Can you handle it?"

I wanted to laugh.

I was like a desert rose now, sprung from those seeds that have to be scorched in fire to bloom. I could handle anything, and that included *typing and taking notes*. It sounded so wholesome—as far from American Apparel as I could get. Exactly the kind of boring corporate job I was looking for.

"I can handle it," I told him.

I started to feel that old ambition spark up again and warm me with its glow. Where had it been hiding these past few years? The girl—no, the woman—from Bryn Mawr had fully arisen. She had her voice back and was ready to take charge of her life again.

I resolved that it was time to leave fashion behind for good.

Really, what had I been *thinking*? The whole industry was toxic and exploitative for women. It preyed on our insecurities, it turned us into objects. It had deep, underlying systemic problems rooted in sexism and capitalism—did I think I was going to beat the system when the house was stacked against me?

But television? Now that was a legitimate career field.

CBS was where *Roseanne* was created, *The Mary Tyler Moore Show*. It was a place for intrepid women, where a fledgling writer like me could thrive. Maybe here I'd find a corporate culture that would see me first as a valued employee, and not just a young woman to be manipulated and sexualized and used. A place where I'd be prized for my smarts over my appearance, my competency over my fuckability.

After all, CBS was a Hollywood institution, a real-deal venerated and vaunted establishment. It wasn't trying to rebel or create a new world order. It wasn't trying to buck the system or fight the Man—it *was* the Man. And it wasn't run by a misogynistic perv like Dov—it was overseen by a wildly successful, highly respected producer and family man named *Les Moonves*. His wife even hosted the show I'd be working on, which boded well for a respectful work environment, right?

As I pulled into the CBS Studio Center lot, I was flooded with hope.

Maybe here it was all going to happen for me.

Maybe behind these gates, I'd finally get a fair shake.

Acknowledgments

Thanks to my family, especially my parents, for their unyielding lifelong support.

Much appreciation for my wise agent, Meredith Miller. Also Byrd Leavell, Olivia Fanaro, Lily Dolin, and Dan Milaschewski at United Talent. Thank you to my brilliant editors, James Melia and Sarah Crichton, and their industrious team at Holt, especially Lori Kusatzky. Additional thanks to Molly Bloom, Shelly Perron, Meryl Levavi, Catryn Sibersack, Laura Flavin, and Sonja Flancher.

Huge thanks to Brett Paesel, Andrew van Baal, Nicky Guerreiro, Julian Chan, Michael K. Cantwell, Marilyn Friedman at Writing Pad, Julia Lee Barclay-Morton and the Inwood NYC Writing Workshop, Anders Lycksell, Collyn Hinchey, Jay Hudak, Liz Eavey, George Germak, and Jennifer Carpinteyro and family.

Gratitude for those who provided me with places free of pestilence to write this book, particularly Christian Sariol at Angeles Crest goat ranch, Ash Maharaj at Harmony Motel in Twentynine Palms, and Jane Conte and Roger Rugletic at Camp Heaven. Many thanks to Spoke Bicycle Cafe in Frogtown and Hoagie Mike's in Edwardsville, Pennsylvania.

Special thanks to my union, the Motion Picture Editors Guild, IATSE Local 700, and my supportive colleagues at *RuPaul's Drag Race* and *The Amazing Race*.

Posthumous gratitude to Charles "Keep A-Knockin'" Connor and family.

Love to all the American Apparel girls.

Photograph Credits

1. Lauren Bloom
2. American Apparel
3. Kate Flannery
4. American Apparel
5. John Maxwell IV
6. Brittany Anderson
7. Found on Sunset Blvd, April 2005 / Courtesy of Kate Flannery
8. American Apparel
9. American Apparel
10. American Apparel
11. Wynn Smith Bubnash
12. Kate Flannery
13. Eric Travis
14. Courtesy of Kate Flannery
15. Eric Travis
16. Justin Wilczynski
17. Kate Flannery
18. Kate Flannery
19. Eric Travis
20. Ray Tang/Shutterstock

About the Author

Kate Flannery was born and raised in northeastern Pennsylvania. She holds a BA in creative writing from Bryn Mawr College and currently works for the Emmy Award–winning *RuPaul's Drag Race*. She is the lead singer and frontwoman for LA's premier Little Richard tribute band, Big Dick. *Strip Tees* is her first book.